The Warden's Niece

'Miss Avery . . . is a born writer for she has made a book of real quality, entertaining, witty and f[illegible]cident and the real stuff of childhoo[illegible]piness, the disappoint[illegible] minutely observed, [illegible]em personality as [illegible]

[illegible]ookmen*

'*The Warde*[illegible]ght: one even laughs [illegible]tory moreover has a salutary mor[illegible] harassed child of our own day; namely that being good at lessons is not the be-all and end-all here, and that to be ourselves is a more glorious aim than to pass examinations.'

Times Literary Supplement

'The author has a keen eye for quirks of character. She also shows a real understanding of children and their ways. What happens is credible and convincing, and the dialogue has a thoroughly genuine ring.'

British Book News

Other titles in Lions

The Book of Three *Lloyd Alexander*
The Black Cauldron *Lloyd Alexander*
The Greatest Gresham *Gillian Avery*
A Likely Lad *Gillian Avery*
Ghostly Encounters *Susan Dickinson*
Ghostly Experiences *Susan Dickinson*
The Moon of Gomrath *Alan Garner*
The Weirdstone of Brisingamen *Alan Garner*
The Owl Service *Alan Garner*
Elidor *Alan Garner*
The Year of the Stranger *Allan Campbell McLean*
Hill of the Red Fox *Allan Campbell McLean*
When Marnie Was There *Joan Robinson*
Charley *Joan Robinson*
No Way of Telling *Emma Smith*
Thursday's Child *Noel Streatfeild*
Caldicott Place *Noel Streatfeild*

and many more

The Warden's Niece

GILLIAN AVERY

with drawings by Dick Hart

COLLINS: LIONS

First published 1957 by William Collins Sons and Co Ltd
14 St James's Place, London SW1
First published in Lions 1974

Printed in Great Britain
by William Collins Sons and Co Ltd, Glasgow

TO MY GODCHILDREN

Julia Chalkley

Robert Portal

Sarah Williams

Contents

CHAPTER ONE

Maria Escapes

THE monitor had written the date – *le 18 mai 1875* – in French on the blackboard, the class was whispering busily and the more nervous girls biting their pencils and thumbing through their atlases in preparation for the first and worst lesson of the day, geography. Maria's neighbour was chattering to the girl behind her. She had no time to spare for Maria, who was new and silent, but at this particular moment Maria did not in the least care. She was wondering what was going to be said about her geography lesson when it was handed back.

'Sshh,' said the monitor, holding open the door with her head craned round it to see down the passage, 'she's coming.' The class rose to their feet and smoothed down their pinafores. Maria felt sick and said to herself over and over again, 'Even this will pass away,' the only line she remembered from a poem she had learned with her governess in the days before Aunt Lucia had sent her to school.

Maria had lived with Great-Aunt Lucia for as long as she could remember, for her parents had died when she was so young that she had no memory of them at all. The house in Bath was very large and still, and Aunt Lucia was very old. But Maria had her French Mademoiselle, and there was a younger girl who came in to share her lessons; she was not particularly lonely. However, Aunt Lucia's advisers, the doctor, the solicitor, the vicar, and their wives – had decided that Maria was leading a most unnatural life cooped up there with only elderly maids and Mademoiselle to talk to, especially now that Claire was going away to school. They had recommended Miss Simpson's school, Semphill House, at a spa town in the Midlands. It was such a healthy place, they said, easy for her to travel back to Bath in the holidays, and there was her uncle, the Warden of Canterbury College, living not very much farther away, at Oxford.

But Maria found school terrifying. After four weeks she still was not sure where she should be at any given time, or what she was supposed to be doing. People pushed her into the right classroom and then forgot about her, except to say, 'Isn't that new girl slow!' She had learned enough about the school, however, to realize that there was great trouble ahead of her in this geography lesson. Miss Ferguson scolded her daily for the untidiness of her hair at breakfast (Mademoiselle had always brushed it before), and for the ink on her hands at tea, and she was not likely to overlook blots on an exercise. Miss Ferguson's face when she swept into the room was stiff with anger, and the monitor shut the door very gently to try to avert some of the coming wrath. The eight girls sat tense while she announced that their preparation had been done exceedingly badly, but one exercise was so bad as to deserve severe punishment, and she would keep that one for comment until the very end. She flung the books back to them with hands that trembled with anger. The pile grew lower and still Maria's name had not been called. Then just one book lay on the table in front of her.

'But this map,' said Miss Ferguson, 'might have been done better by a pig. Never in the whole history of Semphill House has such disgraceful work been handed in. The girl who produced it is not only dirty, ignorant, and unbelievably sluttish – she is also extremely insolent, to expect anyone to accept such work.'

She held up Maria's map of Germany, on which she had been supposed to mark principal towns and industries, without the help of an atlas. It had heavy blots and was smudged where Maria had wept, wondering where the coal and iron deposits were. She had changed her mind several times over these, and then, appalled at the mess, had scrubbed so hard with her india-rubber that she had made a great hole in the paper.

The storm of words went on, and Maria with her jaw locked, gazed at the wall behind Miss Ferguson. She was listening to her no longer. She was the Professor of Greek at Oxford lecturing to a crowded room and calling Miss Ferguson, who was in the audience, sharply to order for lack of attention. Miss Ferguson, made even angrier by seeing not a tear in Maria's eyes, not a single sign that she was sorry, finished up: 'And unless I have that map of Germany by six o'clock tonight, clean, with all the towns in the right places and the industries where they belong, I shall see to it that you wear a label marked "Slut". Perhaps that will bring you to your senses. You will wear it not only in school all this week, but also when you take your Saturday afternoon walk.'

This brought Maria sharply from her Oxford lecture. She was so stunned that she did not hear a word of the rest of the lesson, nor of the lessons that followed; nor did she notice the sideways glances of the other girls to see how she was taking this. She knew it was impossible to escape the punishment, as she could no more produce a correct map of Germany than she could fly through the air. To be labelled for the eyes of all the school to see, and of the town as well! It was a disgrace she could never escape from all the rest of her life. However old she grew, even if she wrote books and became famous, she would still be remembered as the untidy, dirty girl who was called a slut.

'Maria, will you kindly listen,' said one mistress after another as lesson succeeded lesson, and by the time the morning came to an end, Maria found that her evening preparation included some complicated parsing and five compound interest sums, none of which she had the least idea how to tackle.

The other girls had clattered off to eat their fish pie and rhubarb in the dining-room. Maria stood in the dark passage where they kept their coats. She knew she could not swallow a morsel, and besides, in her struggle to get her hair tidy and thus avoid further trouble, she had made herself very late, and everyone would be angry about that. It would be far better to miss lunch altogether; they were not so likely to notice. She sat down on the floor and rested her head against a coat. It came over her that even if she did by some miracle get through today safely, there was all the rest of the week in which she was bound to get into trouble, all the rest of the term, at least six years of it, always trying to catch up, always dreading something, and never being left alone. But the first hurdle was to escape that label 'Slut' and the arithmetic and the parsing that she had not the least idea how to start. She got to her feet and without realizing what she was doing buttoned on her walking boots, and put on her coat and then her hat, and tried to poke in the wandering wisps of hair. Then she walked to the top of the passage and peered into the corridor beyond. The maids were taking in the rhubarb. Maria stole across to the garden door and closed it quietly behind her. The top table in the dining-room, the one Miss Simpson herself presided over, overlooked the drive, so Maria did not pause for a second. She walked briskly down towards the great iron gates and there she was outside. Horror came over her. What was she doing? She could never walk down that drive again, back into school, without being seen, and there would be the most terrible anger, far worse than anything that had overtaken her yet. She moved quickly down the road; when she was out of sight of the school she slackened her pace. Where was she to go now? If only she could get back to Bath, she thought, perhaps Aunt Lucia could write and say she was not well. Perhaps she could even stay there until the next geography lesson was over. Her left hand felt in her coat pocket and clutched the new five-shilling piece that her Uncle Hadden had given her when she had spent a night at Oxford on her way to school. She had tied it up, together with the key that locked her diary, in the corner of a handkerchief to keep it bright, and during the past few weeks had taken it out from time to time and breathed on it and rubbed it when she thought that no one was looking. It was all the money she had and she had no idea how much it cost to go to Bath.

She reached the station without difficulty. The school's Saturday walks took them near it, and Maria, stumbling along with the smallest girl in the school as her partner in the crocodile, had always hoped that a train would pass as they went by.

She waited at the grille of the booking office for a long time. The ticket man had a porter in there with him, and they were both drinking tea and discussing pigeons. When he did finally come over to attend to Maria he was talking to the porter with his head screwed round over his shoulder.

'Please, is there a train to Bath soon?' asked Maria timidly, waiting for the man to say, 'Lor luv us – what's this? A little lady running away from her school?'

But instead he turned his head round to her, and said, 'Why, bless my soul, you are an unlucky young lady. The through train to Bath left half an hour ago.'

'Isn't there another single one?' asked Maria, aghast.

'Not until 1.32 tomorrow,' said the man with relish. 'You *could* do it by changing trains. But I wouldn't. Not if I was you. It'd be much easier if you was a pigeon, eh Bill?' And he turned his head over his shoulder to where the porter had his face buried in a can of tea, and guffawed with laughter.

'Where would I change trains?' Maria asked.

'Oxford and Reading. But it'd be four hours to wait at one and two hours at the other.' He turned round to the porter. 'That bird of 'Orace's I was telling you about, Bill, 'e didn't come in till the next morning, and old 'Orace for-ever carrying on about 'im being the fastest flier in all Warwickshire – for all I told 'im that my Nancy Bell could get in quicker if she called in at all the publics in the county on her way.'

Changing trains. Maria had no idea what it involved, but was certain that she could not do it by herself; not once, let alone twice. But Oxford – that was where Uncle Hadden lived, and perhaps she would be allowed to spend a night there, and he could tell her how to get to Bath the next day. At any rate, it was the only possible course if she was not to go back to the school. So she pushed forward her five-shilling piece nervously. 'Can I have a third-class ticket to Oxford then please? I can get there without changing, can't I?'

She fully expected the man to say, 'Now just what do you think you're up to, giving me five shillings for something that costs seventeen shillings and sixpence? We'd better see the station master about this.'

But he only said, 'Platform 2, 4.10, no change,' and slammed down her ticket and a shilling, two sixpences, and some pennies. That gave her just two hours and five minutes to wait, and she was extremely hungry. Feeling very bold, she walked into the refreshment room and offered one of her pennies for a currant bun, then she crossed over the bridge to Platform 2 and skulked in the Ladies' Third-Class Waiting Room. To try to calm herself she divided her journey into obstacles. Obstacle one was getting to the gates without being seen. Obstacle two was reaching the station, number three buying her ticket. She was safely over these three obstacles. But four was getting on to the right train, five getting out at the right station, six finding her way to Canterbury College. After that was a blank, and what she was going to say to her uncle was best left unthought about.

Several trains came through before the 4.10 clattered in, only ten minutes late, amid great clouds of steam. Maria, in her anxiety not to be stopped by any porter, ran from the waiting-room and clambered into the carriage directly opposite.

'Does this stop at Oxford, please?' she asked the woman sitting by the door. The woman, thin and poorly dressed, with an anxious face, said, without any interest in Maria, that it did, and returned to her own troubles, which involved straightening up and tidying a girl of about fourteen, who seemed to be going to her first place away from her home as a servant.

'You surely look a meagre sight, Lizzie. Why can't you keep your hat straight now? Whatever you're going to do without someone to push you around I just don't know. Sit straight, do.'

But Lizzie just drooped and swallowed hard, and occasionally a tear trickled down her face. She was a plump rosy girl, dressed in a very new blue serge dress and boots that seemed to hurt her.

'Don't you kick them boots against each other, or you'll look like a gipsy before the journey's end. Now don't carry on, love, you'll soon be coming back to see us, looking ever so smart, and there's Uncle Matt who'll come over in the cart from Long Slinfold to see how you're keeping.' And for comfort she produced a huge bundle of brown paper which held bacon sandwiches, a lump of cucumber, and some oranges. Lizzie grew more cheerful at the sight of all this, and Maria felt rather glad that mother and daughter were too absorbed in their own affairs to stare at her and wonder what she was doing.

The train bumped past buttercupped fields, and here and there a child stood in the middle of the buttercups and waved to them. Maria said to herself, 'It's lucky you don't know how much misery there is on this train.' Then she tried to find comfort in the fact that there was still over an hour before she had to face her uncle.

But soon after this she caught sight of a church standing in the middle of the fields, and remembered that on the journey from Oxford this had come fairly soon after they had left the station. Besides, the grey afternoon was beginning to turn into evening, she must have been on the train a long time already. Then Oxford did come into sight, railway sidings, a faint glimpse of church spires, and then they clattered into the station. The great thing, Maria knew, was not to look at a loss. If you hesitated someone would say, 'Well now, little missy, and what are *you* up to?'

So she followed Lizzie, who was now forlornly clutching a bursting paper parcel while her mother struggled with a corded yellow tin trunk. Outside it had begun to rain, a light misty rain that was very penetrating. She hesitated for a moment at the station door and then trotted out, down the slope towards the town, where the gas lamps were beginning to twinkle. She hoped she would remember where Canterbury College was, but she had been driven there in a cab four weeks ago, and though she had paid great attention to the streets they had passed through because she was so excited to be in Oxford at last, it had seemed a confusing route. However, she knew she would be able to recognize the huge clock tower over the main gateway from streets away, if she ever got there without being arrested as a truant from school.

She hurried through the crowds of idly strolling young men who all seemed to be turning back to look at her and laugh. Then there were older people, who looked at her gravely and seemed to discuss her with their companions. There were plenty of houses and shops, but nothing remotely resembled a college building; perhaps after all she had got out at the wrong station. Then she emerged at an immensely broad, tree-lined street where cabs were rattling over the cobbles; and there she heard the Canterbury clock. Slowly and haltingly it chimed those sixteen notes that Uncle Hadden had told her were the opening phrases of an old hymn tune, and hesitated over the last four notes in a way that Maria remembered vividly. She had loved the tune so well that she had always tried to be near the clock tower when it struck the hour, but however hard she had tried to remember them she had always forgotten the curious rise and fall of the notes by the time the next hour came round. On this occasion the Canterbury clock was soon drowned by a chorus of chimes from all over the town, but Maria had heard enough for her to guess the direction. She crossed the broad street and hastened over the wet glistening pavements. It was raining faster now, and she realized for the first time that she had lost her hat. It must have been left behind in the train, or in the waiting-room at the first station. The rain ran down her face and dripped from her eyebrows. She thought she caught a glimpse of the tower, but then it disappeared into a maze of grey buildings. By now she was almost running in her panic, and the lump at the back of her throat which she had been trying to swallow down was almost choking her, and was making her breath come in wheezy gasps. She turned a corner into a narrow street of cobbles, and there near the bottom the great tower of Canterbury College raised itself. Somewhere beyond it, farther down the street, was the front door of the Warden's Lodgings. As she approached the gateway to the college she slowed down and examined the two houses beyond. Which of these was the Lodgings? You could of course reach the house through the college quadrangle, but this was not the entrance that she had used when Mademoiselle had brought her four weeks before; it was probably the Warden's own private entrance. However, a great roar of laughter from a group of young men coming down Canterbury Lane behind her made her shy like a startled horse, and she dashed through the college gateway, a small opening in huge iron-studded gates, past little knots of gossiping young men, into the grassy court beyond. Out of the corner of her eye she saw two bowler-hatted men make a lunge at her, and she heard shouts. But she could see the door she wanted just a few yards away, and she pelted over as hard as she could run.

Inside the Lodgings, the Reverend Henry Henniker-Hadden, Warden of Canterbury College, stood warming himself in front of a wood fire in the library, talking to the Wykeham Professor of Ancient History. Hearing shouts from the quadrangle outside and feet pounding up the gravel paths, the professor looked idly out of the window.

'Dear me,' he said, 'your porters seem to be chasing a little girl.'

The Warden came over. 'Why, bless my soul,' he exclaimed, 'it's my great-niece, Maria,' and he strode to open the door.

Meanwhile, Maria, tugging hard at the bell, had realized that she did not in the least know how she was going to explain herself to Uncle Hadden. But however carefully she had prepared a speech she could never have spoken it; she was so winded. She could only look pathetically at this tall, stooping figure with its iron-grey hair and hooked nose.

'That's all right, Bastable,' said the Warden to the bowler-hatted man who stood nonplussed behind Maria, 'my niece has come to the wrong door.' He shut the door. 'My dear Maria, you seem very wet. You need a glass of sherry wine.' And with that he guided her into the library.

'My niece, Maria,' he said, 'Professor Smith.' He went over to a table carrying an array of decanters, and poured out a glass for Maria.

'Well, well, well,' said Professor Smith, who was rather fat and had a red and friendly face. 'And what have you been up to? Running away from school, eh?'

Maria's face turned bright scarlet, and she nearly dropped the glass her uncle had just handed her.

'It was the geography,' she blurted out, 'I was so bad at it and everyone was so angry. But I only wondered if I could stay here tonight, and then if you can tell me how I get to Bath, I'll go back to Aunt Lucia tomorrow.'

'That,' said Uncle Hadden, 'I am afraid is impossible. I am very sorry to have to tell you that your Aunt Lucia died yesterday. I had just sent Miss Simpson a letter to tell her of this.'

CHAPTER TWO

Thomas, Joshua, and James

THE silence that followed this statement was broken by Professor Smith.

'Why, bless my soul,' he remarked brightly, 'I think the young lady is going to cry.'

But it was not the death of poor Aunt Lucia that had affected Maria. She had only known her as an old, old lady, sitting wrapped in shawls in a darkened room so over-crowded with her favourite pieces of furniture and pictures of her family that Maria used to spend a lot of time when she sat with her trying to make out exactly how many objects the room did contain. She had never counted beyond 150, but there were far more. What had now struck Maria with awful force was that there was no longer anywhere to go, not even in the holidays. She would have to spend every single day of the year under the roof of Semphill House, like poor cowed little Alice Burton whose parents lived in India. However, there is nothing more unpleasant than being told you are going to cry, and so in rage and embarrassment Maria bolted for the hall and tried to open the door into the college quadrangle. Her uncle followed her.

'My dear Maria, I can't have my porters chasing you round the quad again. And you can't get wherever you are going tonight, it's too late. I suggest that you spend the night here in the Lodgings; you seem very wet, and no doubt you are very tired. I'll send my housekeeper to you, and she had better dispatch a telegraph to your school as soon as the post office opens in the morning.'

Maria was shivering with dampness and misery when the formidable Mrs Clomper came to her rescue. Her glass of sherry had been left behind in the library, for which she was very thankful; she had not liked it at all. As Mrs Clomper conducted her disapprovingly up the stairs Professor Smith appeared in the library door and called cheerfully, 'Good night, my dear young lady. I hope you sleep well after all your adventures. I'll send Mrs Smith to you, Warden; she is used to dealing with this sort of scrape. Thomas, Joshua, and James, you know, always in some trouble or other.'

Maria was taken to the room she had slept in before. It overlooked the quad, and was furnished with enormous mahogany chests and cupboards, and a mirror twice her size that swung between two mahogany posts. It stood near the windows, and if you forgot about it and caught sight of your reflection in it unawares, it seemed as though there was another person in the room. Maria saw herself in it now by the light of the oil lamp that Mrs Clomper had brought. She was a bedraggled object; no wonder the porters had chased her. Her face had ink and smuts on it, her hair looked like porcupine quills, and her coat and stockings were heavily splashed with mud.

When Mrs Smith appeared ten minutes later Maria was sitting wrapped in shawls watching a housemaid light a fire, spread towels in front of it, and bring cans of water to fill a hip bath. (The Lodgings possessed no bathroom, nor was there the gaslighting that Maria was used to.) Maria eyed the bath with some anxiety. It would certainly be pleasant to have it in front of the fire, but she did hope she was going to be allowed to have it alone. Mrs Smith did not pay much attention to Maria. She carried two nightgowns and talked breathlessly to Mrs Clomper.

'Oh, Mrs Clomper, I've brought a nightgown for your unexpected visitor. The professor said take one of Master

Maria was shivering with dampness and misery

Joshua's as he is the same age as this little girl. I said I really thought that was rather unsuitable, it would be better for her to have one of mine. But now I see her she does seem so very small that perhaps it will have to be Master Joshua's after all. Luckily I brought it with me.'

Maria looked at the vast Mrs Smith and thought that she would fall out of any nightgown that that lady could lend her. She watched the steam curling up from the bath, and the flames leaping in the fireplace behind. A bath, even one so small as that, would be very nice indeed. Fortunately they both now left her; Mrs Smith was eager to show the cook how to prepare black-currant tea; there was nothing like it, she said, for staving off a chill.

Later on, a housemaid brought her up the black-currant tea, and a lamb cutlet and some apricot tart. After they had taken the tray from her, and it was dark enough for the fire to throw great flickering shadows on the ceiling, Maria crept to the window, pushed it open and leaned out into the open air. The rain had stopped and there was a delicious smell of warm summer earth. Close to her ear the clock chimes began to move through the solemn phrases of the ancient tune, and then behind the vibrating boom of nine o'clock she could hear faintly the chimes of all the other clocks in Oxford. She fell to wondering how many people had listened to those chimes, and had tried to remember the tune years later; and how many people had hurried over those paths below her. Hundreds and hundreds – thousands probably. She wondered whether the undergraduates who walked across the quadrangles were reminded, as she was sure she would be, of the undergraduates who had walked there before them and were now forgotten, and whether they thought that in a few years' time they themselves would be completely forgotten. And she scrambled back into bed almost in tears with the sorrow of it all.

The bell for college chapel woke her, and the sound of many feet scrunching over the gravel paths towards it. The sense of well-being she had had before she had fallen asleep last night had declined, for she realized that there would have to be an interview with Uncle Hadden, followed by a journey back to school. But at least, she reflected, trying to search for comfort, it would make a good entry for her diary, which usually only recorded what there was for lunch, and which people had been cross with her. The trouble was that, once back in Semphill House, she would never be left alone for long enough to write it all down.

Breakfast was brought to her in bed. It was a very good breakfast, coffee instead of the usual tea, an egg in a silver egg cup, and hot rolls. But Mrs Clomper swept into the bedroom in the course of it, carrying Maria's dried clothes.

'I'm very sorry I'm giving you so much trouble,' said Maria meekly.

But Mrs Clomper did not respond as she had hoped with comforting remarks, she merely said, 'The Warden would like to see you in the library at half past nine, Miss Maria.'

Maria dressed and hung round the room until the clock chimed the half-hour. Then she crept downstairs and knocked very timidly at the library door. The Warden was standing by the window, and Maria could not see his face against the light.

'So you dislike your school,' he said, pulling his great hooked nose. 'And what is wrong with it? Too much work? Have they been very harsh with you?'

'I do get into a great deal of trouble,' whispered Maria, staring at her feet.

'And what for?'

'I am very untidy, and nearly always late for things. I never remember to put my house shoes into my shoe bag and that makes them very angry. Miss Simpson told me last

Friday in front of the whole school at lunch time that I was consistently disobedient and careless about it, and strong measures would have to be taken. And I lose my handkerchiefs and don't give my exercise books in, and that makes them very angry too. But chiefly it was because I made a hole in the middle of my map of Germany and Miss Ferguson said I would have to wear a label with "Slut" on it for a week.'

Uncle Hadden came farther into the room. 'And what do they teach you?'

'Parsing and arithmetic,' said Maria, remembering her two last lessons at Semphill House, 'and French and needlework and geography and history. I'm very bad at them all, though I do like history. But the book that we use doesn't like Charles I and I do and Miss Ferguson says I'm wrong.' Maria stopped with a jerk, for she realized she was mumbling and speaking far too fast, and at school they were always reprimanding her for this.

'What sort of lessons would you like?'

'Greek and Latin.' Maria was astonished to hear herself say this. Though she had pored over a battered Greek grammar she had found among the books in Aunt Lucia's house, she had never thought before of anyone teaching it to her. Uncle Hadden lifted one huge grey eyebrow. He looked startled.

'And why Greek and Latin?'

'Because I want to be Professor of Greek in Oxford.' Maria was horrified at this admission she had made. She had blurted out what was only a daydream she had used to comfort herself at school. Uncle Hadden looked considerably more startled. 'Now, why ever should you want that?'

But Maria had no idea herself. The original idea had come from the Greek grammar, when she had laboriously learnt the Greek alphabet and amused herself by writing out

English words in Greek letters. It was the one thing that she could do that her companions at school could not. So she just rubbed the toe of her shoe round a pattern in the carpet and said she did not know.

However, Uncle Hadden seemed interested. He paced up and down with his hands clasped behind his back. 'A very creditable ambition, my dear Maria, and one that I hope to live to see fulfilled. But an establishment for young ladies is no preparation for a chair in Greek. We must have you properly taught. I see no reason why you should not be very apt; your father was a very able young man, and you seem to have inherited the family high forehead – always a good sign. And now that they are admitting female students into Oxford there is every chance that there may be female professors in your lifetime, if not in mine.' He seemed thoroughly excited and was walking at a great pace round the room. 'The next thing is to find you a good tutor. I will speak to Professor Smith about it, I know he has a tutor for his three boys. Of course we shall have to take you away from your school, but as I am now your sole legal guardian there will presumably be no difficulty about that. Young girls should never be sent to schools, incompetent teaching, ridiculous subjects, and all those shrill female voices – terrible.'

Maria stood confused in the middle of the library carpet. 'But where shall I live, Uncle Hadden?' She thought of the huge house in Bath with just herself and the elderly servants.

'Here in the Lodgings – I am afraid this is the only home left to you, you poor child.'

This took Maria considerably by surprise. The Lodgings as a home had never occurred to her.

'Whatever shall I say to him at mealtimes?' she wondered. And if it turned out that she was hopeless at Latin and Greek, would he send her away? More pressing still;

when luncheon came, would he have forgotten her presence altogether? Aunt Lucia used to say: 'Your Uncle Hadden is a very learned man, he does not live in this world at all. It is useless expecting him to deal with day-to-day affairs.'

But on this occasion he seemed to have been very business-like, for over the white wastes of damask tablecloth that stretched between him and Maria at luncheon he said briskly, 'I have arranged for you to have lessons with Professor Smith's three boys. They have an excellent tutor, and as James Smith is just about to make a beginning on Greek and Latin you can start with him. And Mrs Smith has very kindly asked you to take tea this afternoon with the boys.'

Three boys, pondered Maria. It sounded formidable. She looked at Uncle Hadden from time to time, for she would have liked to ask him about the Smiths, but he seemed so deep in thought, his eyes fixed on the tablecloth just beyond his plate, that it would have been an impertinence. It also seemed an impertinence to keep her eyes on him when he was so unconscious of her presence, so she gazed at the wall above his head. Like the rest of the room, it held a yellowing black and white engraving, but unlike the other engravings, which seemed mostly statues and ancient ruined temples, it showed a view of a house. It seemed to have been drawn from the top of a high hill, for it looked down on the house and its gardens and orchards, which lay spread out like a map. The Warden finished his last morsel of Stilton, laid his knife very precisely down the middle of his plate, and raised his eyes. 'Are you interested in my Kips?' he asked, noticing the direction of Maria's gaze. 'It's of little artistic merit, I'm afraid, few of Kips's engravings are, but it's valuable from the architectural point of view. Go over and look at it if it interests you.'

When Maria looked closer she was delighted. There the

house lay, as if it were in a valley below her, with every window shown, every tree in its orchards, every path in the gardens. There were tiny figures of gardeners, of people strolling on the terrace, and of deer wandering in the parkland. It seemed a house of immense size, for beyond the gardens which lay on two sides of the house, were orchards and plantations, and meadows, and then fields and farm buildings, and rolling wooded country beyond.

'Is it real?' she asked.

'Oh, yes,' said the Warden. 'It's Jerusalem House, which is quite near Oxford. When Kips drew it at the end of the seventeenth century it was at the height of its fame – though the people who lived in it then were not so interesting as they had been a couple of generations before in Charles I's reign. The then Lord Fitzackerley entertained all the learned men of England there, and laid out new gardens, and searched Europe for art treasures. You must go there and see the house for yourself.'

This last remark, as Maria knew from experience, meant very little on the lips of one's elders, and she soon forgot it. But at every meal she gazed at the engraving, trying to imagine what it would be like if she was actually there, walking on the terrace or in the gardens.

Mrs Clomper tied on her bonnet for the purpose of escorting Maria to the Smiths' front door. They left the Lodgings by the proper door, that opened on to Canterbury Lane, and walked perhaps fifteen yards, not more, down to the front door of the next house. Though Maria when she had been running down the lane the night before had thought the two houses were so alike as to be indistinguishable, she saw now that they were quite different. The Smiths' house was much taller for one thing, it had three stories where the Lodgings only had two. As Maria raised her eyes to take this in, she saw in a second floor window a face flattened against the glass; a voice floated down, 'It's the girl.' Then the face disappeared with some suddenness and a little shriek. The curtains moved and portions of two more faces appeared at the sides. Mrs Clomper waited until Maria was safely over the threshold, and then left her with a warning: 'I shall call for you at six o'clock, Miss Maria, and mind you are ready for me. I don't want any dilly-dallying.'

The maid who had opened the door escorted Maria to Mrs Smith, who conducted her up the stairs. As they walked along the first landing there was a sound of scuffling and heavy breathing overhead and something fell down in front of them. Maria snatched at it and caught it before it fell. It seem to be a sort of homemade spider on the end of a piece of cotton. Mrs Smith apparently did not notice. She was talking agitatedly about the tutor: 'He's a clergyman, you know, such a very clever man but so very High Church, and must have fish for luncheon on Fridays which is tiresome and annoys cook.'

When they arrived in the schoolroom there were three boys drawn up in a line with expressionless faces. One was taller than Maria, with black hair, one was about her own age, and there was a small plump one covered with freckles, with red hair that curled all over his head.

'Thomas, Joshua, and James,' said Mrs Smith rapidly. 'Thomas is thirteen, Joshua is eleven, and James is eight, and this is Maria, the Warden's little niece. James, you have not been making ink pellets again, after all Papa said to you! Just look at your hands!'

'No, it was a spider this time,' said James agreeably, looking at his hands and wiping them on his trousers. 'The girl picked it up. Can I have it back, please?'

'That's a rotten spider, James,' remarked the eldest boy as Maria handed it over, 'and anyway it's got too many legs.'

'Well, I'm sure I don't know why you want to go making spiders especially after Papa has just given you a rabbit. Now look after Maria, and don't fight, and James, wash your hands.' Mrs Smith disappeared from the schoolroom.

'Didn't the spider frighten you at all?' asked James gloomily.

There were three boys drawn up in a line

'How could it?' said the tall boy. 'It doesn't even look like a spider – it's got eleven legs.'

'Well, she's a girl,' said James cuttingly. 'Most of them are frightened by anything. Do you know you're the first girl that has ever come to tea in the schoolroom? The usual ones have tea in the dining-room.'

'That's because so few of them ever come,' said Joshua hurriedly, in case Maria should be hurt. 'There was the

Bishop's granddaughter and she had tea in the dining-room because she came with her mother.

'Oh, she was silly,' said James reflectively, 'and her name was Arabella!'

They stood and looked at Maria, and she looked back with some nervousness. The eldest one, Thomas, seemed far older than she, and very aloof. He probably despised girls. The middle one, Joshua, appeared more approachable. He was small and pale and had a friendly face. But the red-headed James with his determined expression was going to be a great trial. As far as she knew, she had never spoken to a boy in her life, except the ones she had had as partners at her dancing classes at Bath, and then there had been no more conversation than 'I'm afraid I trod on your foot just then.' 'Oh, no, it was my fault really.'

She had no idea what she was going to say to the Smiths.

'We've seen you already,' remarked James after he had stared at her for a long time.

'I saw you too,' said Maria. 'You were looking out of the window.'

'Oh, long before that,' said Thomas in a bored way. 'We could see you in the Warden's garden.'

'You were swinging on a branch of one of his apple trees,' put in James. 'We saw you.'

Maria blushed to think that all her movements this morning had been scrutinized. Had she done anything else that they might laugh at, she wondered? Joshua went over to the window.

'Look how much you can see of his garden.'

The two gardens lay side by side, a high wall dividing them, and unless you were directly under this wall in the Lodgings garden it would be difficult to avoid being seen from the schoolroom window. There was a great difference between the two sides of the wall. On the Lodgings side the lawn was velvety green, the flowerbeds were filled with lines of flowers like well-drilled soldiers, and a row of equally well-drilled fruit trees screened off the orderly kitchen garden. But the Smiths' lawn had bare tracks in it, and instead of flowerbeds under the wall there was, about half-way down, a henhouse and wired-in run where the hens were scratching.

'It would really be much easier to climb over the wall to get here,' exclaimed Maria. 'That row of fruit trees across Uncle Hadden's garden would stop me being seen by Mrs Clomper.'

'That's what the undergraduates do,' said James, 'when they want to get back into college after it's locked.'

'It makes Papa so angry,' said Joshua. 'They climb over our garden gate, and then get up on the wall from our hen-house and jump into the Warden's garden, and climb over his other wall into the college. And getting up on the hen-house always wakes the hens, who make a most terrible noise and wake Papa.'

'It's being woken up that he minds,' added Thomas, 'not the undergraduates. But Papa's a great sport, you know. I heard the Warden saying once that he simply couldn't understand why there were so often deep footmarks in his border. "And the curious thing is," he said, "that the foot-prints always point away from the wall, never towards it." '

Maria thought this was a very good imitation of her uncle's voice. 'And what did your father say?'

'He just said, "Well, gardeners are curious fellows, my dear Warden." '

'It was very clever of him to say that,' put in Joshua, 'because it wasn't untrue, but it made him think of gardeners, not undergraduates.'

'Will you come over the wall when you come in to lessons?' asked James.

'That's a good idea,' said Joshua. 'Thomas, couldn't you make a rope ladder? You said you might so that we could climb the pear tree by the henhouse more easily.'

'I dare say I could.' Thomas looked as though nothing would induce him to do so.

Maria's thoughts were more on the tutor, however, than how to climb in and out of the Smiths' garden. 'Do you all have lessons with Mr Ledgard?'

'Joshua does,' said Thomas, 'and I will until the end of this term. I go to Rugby in September. Papa won't send us to school before we go to Rugby, he says private schools are just expensive nonsense and that we learn far more with a tutor.'

'I'm going to have lessons with Mr Ledgard too,' said James, glaring defiance.

'Oh, yes, James has been promoted to lessons with Mr Ledgard, you will have to share them with him. He had a governess until last week, she came in every morning, but he has just driven her away.'

'Poor Miss Gracie,' said Joshua. 'She used to teach Thomas and me once, but James nearly drove her mad, and Papa said he was not going to expose any more female nerves to him.'

'She was so silly,' complained James. 'She wouldn't argue. She just said, "Be quiet, James", all the time. But you ran away from school, didn't you?' He looked Maria up and down. 'Papa said so at breakfast.'

For the second time in five minutes Maria blushed. James watched her with interest. 'Goodness, you do go red. Are you going to run away from Rugby, Thomas? I expect Joshua will when he goes. He always gets homesick. Do you remember when he went to Aunt Anna's how Papa had to go and fetch him home?'

'That's enough, James.' Thomas gave him a push and then turned to Maria. 'How did you get here? By train?'

'Yes. It was very easy really,' mumbled Maria.

'It must be lovely, going in a train by yourself.' James was unquenchable. 'You can lean out of the windows as much as you like and needn't shut them when you go through tunnels, so you can smell the lovely tunnel smell. When I go to school I shall sit with all the windows open and I shan't care what anybody else in the carriage says.'

'I expect they'll send Nurse with you to see you don't fall out, you silly little boy.'

'Nurse!' said James with a look of scorn.

She came in at that moment with a teapot, followed by a maid carrying a loaded tray, and swept James off to wash the ink from his hands.

'I pity you having to have lessons with him,' said Joshua. 'He never stops talking.'

'But you'll get used to him,' said Thomas in a friendly way that Maria found flattering. 'After a little you just stop hearing what he says. The great thing is not to argue with him. He always has the last word.'

'It was the arguing that made Papa decide that he had better start lessons with Mr Ledgard. Mr Ledgard is much better at it than Miss Gracie. Anyway Miss Gracie wanted to teach some girls.'

'I wouldn't like to teach girls,' said Maria, 'they giggle, and when somebody scolds them they cry.'

Thomas looked at her with what seemed to be approval. 'Don't you like girls?'

'No,' said Maria with great emphasis, remembering the abject obedience of the girls in the Semphill House classrooms and their 'Oh, Miss Ferguson', and 'Please, Miss Ferguson', and their high-pitched sniggerings afterwards.

As Joshua had warned, James talked all the way through tea, but nobody paid any attention, least of all Nurse. She was an old wrinkled woman, so old that she must have been nurse to Professor Smith, but she did not seem in the least put out by James. James suddenly interrupted his remarks about trains and asked, 'What would *her* name be on a tomb?'

Nobody seemed startled at this except Maria.

'It would stay the same, of course,' said Thomas witheringly. 'Maria couldn't possibly be shortened.'

'Poor thing,' said James, attacking his sponge cake again.

'I don't suppose Miss Maria wants her name changed,' said Nurse. 'Such silliness talking about tombs at your age.'

James took no notice. 'Thomas is Thos, Joshua is Jos., and I am Jas. Jas is the best name.'

Joshua looked at Thomas. 'Can't you stop him?'

'Take no notice of him, do,' said Nurse. 'You know it only makes him worse. Now, Master James, you stop being so silly, and don't lick your fingers.'

'Papa takes us out visiting country churchyards,' said Thomas, turning his back on James, 'and we always look at the inscriptions on the tombs. Sometimes they are in Latin, but mostly they're in English, and they often shorten the names – "Thos Browne, knight, of this parish".'

' "Jas Smith, a gent of great hopes who died young". That's what it said on one we saw last Saturday. I wonder if that Jas Smith was anything like me.'

'He wouldn't have had jam on his fingers,' said Nurse. 'Now you just drink up your milk and be quiet.'

But it was impossible to stop James once he was wound up. 'I want my tombstone to be in English, not Latin, so that everyone can see how good I was, and how sad it was that I died.'

His brothers looked at him in deep disgust. 'Good heavens, James,' said Thomas, 'nobody in their senses could bring themselves to write an epitaph for you in Greek, Latin, or English.'

'Except one which just said "J. E. Smith",' added Joshua.

'They could if they were paid,' said James.

'There's a gravestone in a church near Bath,' said Maria hurriedly to distract them, 'which says, "What is life without a mother? Peace, perfect peace".'

Thomas was convulsed with laughter, but it reminded Joshua of something else. 'It was terrible at breakfast yesterday. James called Mamma an old harridan.'

'I didn't. I just said, was she an old harridan? It was something I had read in a book. I wanted to know what it meant.'

'It came to the same thing. It upset her a lot.'

'It seemed to upset Papa more,' said James musingly, 'he beat me in the study, but it didn't hurt at all, really. "Peace, perfect peace". I'll tell Mamma that.'

'No, you're not to,' said Maria, horrified.

'No, James, you must promise not to; poor Mamma.' Joshua was very upset.

'What will you give me if I promise? Will you give me your chocolate biscuit? You can have my piece of bread and butter, if you like.'

'Now, now, Master James. We've had quite enough nonsense from you for one day. You know you've got to eat that piece of bread and butter and you're having no more chocolate biscuits.'

'I'm going to call myself Jas in future. It's a very good name. And you had better call yourselves Thos and Jos.'

Maria, when she got home that evening, wrote up the day's events on a piece of paper to be gummed into her diary when her trunk came from school. About the Smiths she wrote: 'Thomas is very clever, I think, but seems very grown-up. I should like him to like me, but I am afraid he despises me because I must seem so silent and stupid. Joshua has very good manners. He wants to please people, which irritates Thomas, who does not care. James has red hair. He is OUTRAGEOUS. If he was my brother I should fight him all the time.'

The three Smiths also kept diaries; their father had pointed out to them that the one certain way of being famous after they were dead was to keep a journal. 'You may not live to know it, my dear boys, but think what a gold mine these diaries will prove to your grandchildren, who will make enormous sums publishing them. And, of course, when you come to write your autobiographies, as I am sure you all will, they will be most useful.'

Thomas wrote: 'Papa has foisted the Warden's niece on us to share lessons with Mr Ledgard. She is thin and brown and silent, but rather better than most girls.'

Joshua wrote: 'We had a girl to tea. James behaved very badly. Thomas and I are sure when he grows up he is going to disgrace the family. It is lucky Smith is a common name.'

James wrote: 'A girl came to tea. There were chocolate biscuits. I do not think she will be famous so her name does not matter.'

CHAPTER THREE

Mr Copplestone Falls into the Henhouse

THE arrangement was that Maria should go to the Smiths' house at 9.30 each morning, have lessons with the boys, and then lunch with them. She should take a walk with them during the afternoon, have a final lesson, and then return to the Lodgings for tea with the Warden. This and breakfast were the only meals which she was to have with him during the week, but even so she thought it was an ordeal.

However, at this first breakfast, Uncle Hadden was concealed behind *The Times*, and did not offer nor expect any conversation. The difficulty was that he propped the paper against the sugar basin, so that Maria had to drink her coffee unsweetened. When a maid came in with the post and he put down his paper, Maria seized her chance and manipulated the heavy tongs to give herself one lump. The maid seemed very young and ill at ease, as if it were the first time she had been sent into the dining-room.

'I think this one's for the young lady,' she said, trying to extricate the bottom letter from the pile. The Warden glanced at it, and then at Maria with some surprise, and handed it back to the maid. Maria, struggling to release the sugar from the tongs into the cup before Uncle Hadden returned to *The Times* and shut off the sugar basin, looked up at the maid. To her astonishment she saw the Lizzie who had sat opposite her in the train. Lizzie was in a state of great confusion and did not meet her eyes; she just handed Maria a piece of paper folded and heavily sealed, which said 'Strictly Private'.

'Come as early as you can,' she read, 'we have something to show you. There is a new tutor, Mr L. has had to go away.'

Mrs Smith had told Maria to go round by the back gate, into the house by the garden door, and make her own way up to the schoolroom. She did this with much nervousness. Would Mrs Smith have remembered to tell the household to expect her to come in this way, or would they wonder who in the world she was? She hovered in the passage by the garden door listening to the clattering of dishes and the sound of voices in a distant kitchen, trying to raise courage to make a bolt for the schoolroom. She shrank back against the overcoats hanging on the pegs as a door opened and somebody strode out into the hall and towards the passage.

'Aha,' said Professor Smith, 'early and eager for lessons, I have no doubt. But there is a disappointment for you, I fear. We have temporarily had to replace Mr Ledgard with another clerical gentleman – the Reverend Francis Copplestone. But a temporary measure only, I hope; Mr Copplestone is too tall for my comfort, poor fellow, poor fellow.'

'Shall I go up to the schoolroom?' asked Maria nervously, hoping that he would offer to take her up himself.

'Thom-as, Josh-ua,' called the professor at the top of his voice. There was a pause, then a door was opened, and feet banged down the top flight of stairs.

'Come and collect Maria,' he trumpeted. 'She's down here and too nervous to come up by herself.'

It was Joshua who finally rescued Maria. 'Thomas is making a rope ladder,' he panted as he ran up the stairs ahead of her. 'We wanted you to come and see because you'll have to use it. Did you get my note? I pushed it into the Lodgings before breakfast. We've been up since seven o'clock.'

Inside the schoolroom door they had to step over James, who was lying on the floor on his stomach.

'I've got to blow this marble hard enough to knock down that cow before I can get up from the floor,' he said, without looking up. 'Joshua, don't tread on the cow or I'll bite your leg. I hope I can blow it down before lessons start or I'll have to stay here – I've vowed to.'

At the table Thomas was working at a garish mixture of red, blue, and white pieces of cloth. Maria and Joshua stood beside him silently.

'It's a pity the knots show so much,' ventured Joshua.

'The main thing is that the knots are strong. You can't expect anything much better from rag-bag pieces.'

'I think its very ingenious,' said Maria.

'Do you think anybody will want the pieces again?'

'Joshua, for goodness' sake don't be so gloomy. If anybody wants the pieces they'll have to unplait the ladder, and then they'll find all the material is in strips so I shouldn't think they'll bother. Come and help me put in another rung. I hope you measured the wall right.'

'Is it for the wall between our two gardens?' asked Maria.

'Yes, it's to save having to come round by the road. My idea is that we tie it to our pear tree that overhangs your uncle's garden, then you would have to climb up it to the top of the wall, pull it up after you, and then if you can't jump down you could swing the ladder to our side of the wall and climb down. You had better help finish it off, otherwise it won't be ready by the time Jos and I have to go down to Papa; we've got to have some lessons with him.'

Maria looked anxiously at the complicated plait of blue serge mixed with white strips from a shirt, and pieces of red flannel, into which pieces of firewood had been cunningly interlaced for rungs. She fumbled with the loose ends of material. 'Is this how I knot it round the wood?'

'If anyone trod on that they would fall into the henhouse. You do it, Jos. Add some more blue stuff to the top, Maria, so that we can tie it to the tree.'

'I've knocked down the cow,' announced James from the floor, 'now I can get up.'

'You had better knock down another one,' said his elder brother.

'I don't want to. I want to help you. What a queer looking thing. The red flannel is from Nurse's petticoat. Is the ladder for the wall? It's much too short.'

Maria was suddenly reminded of something. 'Your father says there is a new tutor and that he is very tall. Have you seen him yet?'

Thomas tied the last knot with great deliberation. 'If these knots don't hold then nothing will. Mr Copplestone? Papa says he's eight foot tall. I must say I'm longing to see. Mr Ledgard had to go off yesterday in a great hurry to take over his father's parish. His father is a clergyman too, and he fell off a ladder looking for owls or something.'

'It wasn't owls,' interposed Joshua, 'it was birds' nests; his father is an ornithologist.'

'Well, it was something pretty silly for a man of his age, and Papa had to find somebody at once. So it's this Mr Copplestone. Nobody knows anything about him except that he's the tallest man ever seen in Oxford.'

'And here is Mr Copplestone in person,' said the professor, flinging open the door. Joshua bundled the ladder into the toy chest behind him and sat on the lid with a guilty expression. The tallest and thinnest man they had ever seen ducked his head uneasily to get through the door, and stood smiling at his feet.

'Here are your four pupils,' the Professor waved his hand

in their direction. 'Thomas and Joshua are going to read the classics with me to give you a free run with the beginners, James here, and Maria.'

Mr Copplestone looked sideways at the children and dropped his eyes again. 'How do you do, Miss Maria? And is Master James the auburn-hued gentleman?'

Joshua gave a nervous look at James to see how he took this. James was gazing with fascination at the snaky length of Mr Copplestone. 'Are you really eight feet tall, and how tall were you when you were my age?'

'Now, now, James,' said his father, 'not so many tiresome questions. Come along, Joshua, come along, Thomas, we'll deal with Virgil downstairs, and leave Mr Copplestone to explain the mysteries of *mensa* to your brother. Bring your books with you.' The door closed behind them.

'I know *mensa*,' said James cuttingly.

'And so you should,' said Mr Copplestone, lifting his eyes from his feet, which he was arranging in dancing positions. 'The son of John Evelyn the diarist could read English, Latin, and French at the age of two and a half, and at the age of four could turn English into Latin and had a strong passion for Greek. But then, of course, he died when he was five. You are obviously cut out for a long life.' And he sighed.

James was offended. 'Well, I'm sure Maria doesn't know *mensa*.'

'She is a girl. Girls can start later because they work so much harder. It's terrible trying to make a boy work.' Mr Copplestone sighed again and pointed to his toe. He looked up suddenly at Maria. 'Do you know, I have never spoken to a little girl before in my life. They frighten me.'

Maria did not know what to say to this. James had no difficulty. 'I've spoken to hundreds. They don't frighten me. Why do they frighten you?'

'They look so serious and motherly, or else they giggle. And what does one talk to them about? I don't know anything about dolls.'

'I don't like dolls,' Maria assured him, 'I never did.'

'Well,' said Mr Copplestone, giving a sudden caper across the floor, 'that's a link we all have in common. I'm sure Master James doesn't like dolls either. I like bull-fighting myself, do you?' He swung round to James.

'I've never done any, but I should like to try. I bet I would be awfully good at it.'

'Oh, I've done none, of course. My height, you know, and besides, you have to be a Spaniard to be any good at it. However, I know all the strokes. I practise a little cape-play every morning before breakfast.'

'Show us some, now,' demanded James eagerly.

'If we can get through the first chapter in your Greek grammar by ten-thirty, and Miss Maria can repeat the first and second Latin declensions I'll demonstrate a veronica for you.'

Thus it came about that when Joshua and Thomas flung themselves up the stairs from their father's study to share a history lesson with the two others they found the table pushed back against the window, and the enormous length of Mr Copplestone lunging round the room in a swirl of black clerical coat-tails, using the green plush tablecloth as a cloak to thrust into the face of an imaginary bull.

'This is what happens just before the bull is killed,' shrieked James from the table where he was standing. 'Come and see.'

Mr Copplestone finished his complicated movements and flung down the tablecloth. He gazed round at the disorder he had created in the room but apparently did not notice it. 'Not exactly as the immortal Guerra would have executed it, perhaps, but fair enough – I'm really quite pleased

The enormous length of Mr Copplestone lunging round the room

with myself. Are you interested in the sport?' he asked Joshua.

'I think it's very cruel,' said Joshua indignantly.

'Cruel?' Mr Copplestone bit his finger reflectively. 'No, I don't really think so. No worse than rat-catching or fox-hunting, you know, and so much prettier and more skilful. You should see the matador bowing to the lady of his fancy. So,' and picking up the tablecloth he swirled it round him and bowed elaborately to Maria. 'Now can you imagine a rat-catcher bowing to his audience? Nor can I. What are you expecting me to teach you now? History is it? Very well, let's make a start. You can write what you know about the Wars of the Roses, Miss Maria, Thomas about Napoleon, Joshua about the Reformation, and the auburn-haired gentleman on the table can take Machiavelli. I'll give you twenty minutes, and whoever writes the most, provided it's correct, will get a reward. Each proper name correctly used scores three marks.'

'But I've never heard of Machiavelli,' said James, scarlet with indignation, 'I'm only eight.'

'Never mind, my boy, the luck of the draw, you know. Have you all got pencil and paper? All right, then. On your marks, get set, go.'

There was a scramble for writing tools, and then a pen hurtled by Mr Copplestone's right ear and a rubber hard by his left. James sat rigid in his chair with his face flaming with fury. His brothers looked at him in consternation; no Smith had ever behaved like this. Mr Copplestone bent to pick up the pen and the rubber. 'Your pen, I think, my dear fellow. You'll need this for your essay. I should begin by writing the subject at the top of the page. It helps to promote ideas.' And he went over to the window and looked out humming.

James sulkily did this, and then looked broodingly at Mr

Copplestone's back. 'Do names of books count three marks?' he asked.

'Certainly.'

Maria, bending over the paper and trying to distinguish Lancastrians from Yorkists very unsuccessfully, and getting the battles thoroughly mixed up with the Roundheads and Cavaliers, heard James scratching busily away on his exercise book and scraping his pen round the ink pot. Obviously he had found something to write.

'Time,' announced Mr Copplestone. 'Now you can each read out your essay one by one; the rest of us will correct your mistakes. Then add up the number of proper names you have scored, minus mistakes, and whoever gets most will be rewarded. Thomas, you start.'

Thomas did fairly well with Napoleon, Maria, as she suspected, had mixed up the Wars of the Roses with the Civil War, Joshua had not been able to produce much information about the Reformation. James was triumphant. 'I've won, I've got far more words than Thomas.'

'How do you know they're correct, you silly little boy?' said Thomas heatedly.

'Of course they are.'

'Go on then, read them out.'

James began: 'What do I know about Mackervelly. Nothing. I know he was not a King of England, he was not Henry I, Henry II, Henry III . . .' When James had exhausted all the kings of England he knew he started on the titles of books. 'Mackervelly did not write the Bible, *Pilgrim's Progress*, *Robinson Crusoe*, *The Fairchild Family*, *Hamlet* . . .' and then the battles. 'Mackervelly did not win the Battle of Hastings, the Battle of Agincourt, the Battle of Waterloo, the Battle of Trafalgar. I didn't have time to write any more than that, but it comes to thirty-one names, and that's far more than Thomas.'

His brothers' indignation burst out. 'James, you cheat!' 'Sir, you can't let him get away with that!' 'No, sir, you mustn't, it's terribly bad for him.'

Mr Copplestone nodded his head with great emphasis. 'All perfectly correct information. That boy will go far. I prophesy a great career for him as a rather shady politician.'

'One of the great rogues of history,' muttered Thomas.

'What's my reward?' asked James smugly.

'Sixpence. I have no doubt that you will lend this sum to some unfortunate person at enormous interest and lay the foundations of your fortune on the proceeds.'

'No, I shan't. I shall buy a ha'porth of dolly mixture for the next twelve days. That way I shall get hundreds and hundreds of sweets, enough to have for years.'

'I think we can now say that lessons for the morning are over.' Mr Copplestone consulted an exceedingly small watch. 'Do you think you can tell me what it was you were so busy hiding when I came into the room? I'm afraid I have such a curious nature.' He smiled wistfully with his head on one side.

'It was a sort of ladder,' said Joshua in confusion. Thomas looked at him piercingly, and Joshua grew more confused.

'Oh?' said Mr Copplestone. 'What for?'

Joshua eyed Thomas with alarm. 'For between the gardens,' he blurted out.

'No good expecting Joshua to keep anything to himself,' muttered Thomas savagely to Maria.

'Is it in this chest? Do let me see it.' Mr Copplestone put his hand on the lid and looked inquiringly at Joshua who very reluctantly and with apologetic glances at Thomas helped him to haul it out and pick off the lead soldiers and a bit of a fort which had become tangled in it. Mr Copplestone looked at it with admiration. 'How pretty it is, and those jolly little knots! Would it hold me, do you think?'

'We haven't tried whether it will hold any of us,' Joshua told him.

'Why not try now? We can call the lesson "natural science".'

So they took it down to the garden, James hopping excitedly in front, and Thomas with a remote expression following at the rear. Joshua walked beside him anxiously. 'I really am very sorry, but I couldn't have stopped him, could I?'

Thomas shrugged. Obviously he thought that anybody else could have done it.

'Oh, Thos . . . I am so very sorry,' moaned Joshua. 'Still, it is a good idea to try it out, isn't it?'

They went down the garden towards the henhouse. About two yards from it, surrounded by bare trampled earth which looked as thought the Smiths spent a lot of their time playing there, was a pear tree. In its upper reaches it was easy to climb, but its lowest branch was about six feet up, so that a ladder or something like it was needed to start one off. The branch where Thomas was planning to hang his ladder was about two feet above the wall, and overhung both gardens. Joshua looked at it anxiously. 'I'm sure I forgot to add on a bit to allow for the branch being above the wall when I did the measuring. I think I only measured the wall. Oh, Thomas, I'm sure the ladder's too short.'

Thomas put his hands on his lips and looked at Joshua with contempt. 'I don't know how anybody can be so incompetent as you are. How do you think we're going to lengthen it? We have used up most of the rag-bag as it is.'

'Perhaps we could buy a little bit of rope?'

'If you provide the money. However, as we have got Mr Copplestone here we might as well make use of him.' He caught up the tutor. 'This is the pear tree, sir. If you could give me a leg up I could tie the ladder on to the branch.'

Mr Copplestone hoisted Thomas on to the lowest branch of the tree and then handed up the ladder after him. 'And how are you proposing to attach the object?'

'I thought if I hooked the top rung over these two stubs it would hold,' said Thomas, reaching up to them.

'They look extraordinarily fragile to me. However, you probably know best,' said Mr Copplestone. 'I can offer you some string, if you wish.' He fumbled in his pocket and produced some thin and rather tangled twine. 'It came this morning round a parcel of books on the breeding of budgerigars. It appears that you can make a fair profit on the game, and I am thinking of taking it up. Is the string any use to you?'

Thomas out of courtesy tied it round the top rung and then round the branch. The ladder now hung parallel to the wall, but a foot away from it. It was, as Joshua had gloomily prophesied, a good three feet too short. James was the first to point this out. 'The only person who can use it is Mr Copplestone.'

'And that being so I must be the first person to try it.' Watched by Thomas from the top of the wall and by the other three from below, Mr Copplestone gingerly raised his right foot high enough to reach the bottom rung. He looked like somebody mounting an enormously tall and restless horse. He put in his second foot, and the ladder swayed and swung alarmingly as he crouched at the bottom. James jumped up and down in ecstasy. 'Doesn't Mr Copplestone look like that picture of a spider monkey in my book!'

With a great effort Mr Copplestone managed to straighten himself and put his foot on the second rung. It only needed one more step and he could clamber up on to the wall. Thomas jumped down to make way for him.

'It's splendid up here,' called Mr Copplestone, promenading up and down. 'Such a marvellous view of the Warden's garden – I had always wanted to see it. And who would that female be with a face like a thundercloud who is scowling at me so ferociously from a first floor window?'

'Goodness, that must be Mrs Clomper,' said Maria. aghast. 'Can she see me?'

'No, I am sure she cannot. I'll wave to her and perhaps that will sweeten her. It probably only needs a little kindness to bring her round. It's a very good ladder, Thomas, my boy, a most useful contrivance.'

'But you didn't get up it properly,' objected Joshua, 'you only stepped on two rungs.'

'Very well, I'll come down and go up it step by step. Do you think the professor's henhouse will hold me? It ought to, I am told it has borne generations of young men from Canterbury.' And he jumped down on to it.

There was a sharp crack, a desolate sound of breaking wood, and Mr Copplestone was waist deep in the henhouse with the hens scattering in all directions round their enclosure, squawking wildly. The children were silent with horror.

'This is most uncomfortable,' said Mr Copplestone, 'and most unfortunate, because I am utterly unable to move.'

'Joshua,' said Thomas, 'you'll have to find Papa and tell him what has happened and try not to let Mamma know; it will get her into such a state. And don't say anything about rope ladders, I'll throw it over on to the Warden's side.'

The professor, that moment returned from a lecture, and still in his gown, came striding down the path with Joshua running anxiously beside him. 'What new violence have my wretched hens had to endure? They have already had three broken nights in succession, and now this. Oh, Mr Copplestone, it's you. How in the world did you get yourself into this predicament?'

'An experiment in natural science, Professor, which I insisted on conducting. I can only say how sorry I am, and hope that your natural anger will not condemn me to remain in this henhouse, for I cannot get out without help.' The upper half of Mr Copplestone looked very dejected, and he hung his head like a scolded spaniel.

'I certainly will do my utmost to get you out. Imagine the effect your legs must be having on my poor hens!'

The tender-hearted Joshua was doing his best to comfort them, but he would only give them half his attention because he was sure Mr Copplestone was in great agony. 'Papa, how can we get him out? It must be hurting him dreadfully.'

Professor Smith went to the side of the henhouse. 'I think if he put his weight on me he might be able to extricate himself.'

'Do you think you squashed any hens when you went down?' asked James as Mr Copplestone dragged himself clear.

'No, he didn't, I've counted them,' said Joshua, 'they're all here. But where are they going to sleep tonight?'

'I think Thomas and the gardener will have to attend to that between them. If Thomas can construct a hutch for rabbits he can certainly repair a henhouse.'

The four children stood by the ruins in a dejected huddle, watching the absurd length of Mr Copplestone towering above the professor as they walked back to the house, his neck twisted down uncomfortably as he continued to apologize.

'Now look what your incompetence has brought us to,' said Thomas, rounding on Joshua who looked at him with frightened eyes. 'It will take me weeks to repair this thing, and I suppose Papa will stop money for it out of our pocket money.'

Maria felt this was hardly fair. 'It was Mr Copplestone's fault, really. He made Joshua show him the ladder, and then wanted to try it.'

'Mr Copplestone!' said Thomas, his rage turning to a new object. 'I think he's escaped from a luntatic asylum.'

'He's very kind,' protested Joshua.

'But mad,' said Thomas. 'I hope Mr Ledgard comes back soon, I must say, or goodness knows what other trouble we won't be landed in. And James, I've never known you behave so badly as you did this morning. There would have been terrible trouble if Papa had known. I'm not going to tell him, but as a punishment you can't use this ladder for a week.'

'I'll let you have a pennyworth of dolly mixture if you will,' begged James.

'And I won't have you trying to bribe me out of your ill-gotten gains.'

'We were very lucky that Papa didn't notice the ladder,' said Joshua.

'I'm sure Mrs Clomper did,' said Maria gloomily, 'she notices everything, and she couldn't help seeing Mr Copplestone on the wall waving his arms around. She told me yesterday that I was not to go rampaging with those noisy little boys and disturb the Warden.'

'That's outrageous,' said Thomas indignantly. 'It's our garden, and besides I'm sure the Warden's work isn't nearly as important as Papa's. Anyway, nobody could object to the ladder, we haven't done any damage to it.'

'Could we pull it over on to your side, though?' begged Maria. 'It's so awfully noticeable from the Lodgings, and somebody's bound to see it and ask me about it.'

'You'll have to throw it over from your side of the wall. There's nothing I can do about it from this side.'

'All right, I'll go now,' said Maria fidgeting with anxiety.

'Here comes Mr Copplestone, I'm going to call him the Streak,' announced James.

Mr Copplestone was hurrying towards them, his face happy again.

'My dear young people, all is very well. Your father has agreed to accept the assistance of a carpenter of my acquaintance to repair the henhouse, and as a small compensation to yourselves for the anxiety and distress I have no doubt caused you, I have proposed to him that I should take you up the river to visit the great house of Jerusalem next week. It can be a history lesson.'

'He may be mad, but he does his best,' admitted Thomas later.

'I think he's going to be rather a responsibility,' said Joshua.

CHAPTER FOUR

'An Unknown Boy'

LESSONS with Mr Copplestone were not lacking in interest. Every morning after an hour of Latin and an hour of Greek he would give Maria and James a bull-fighting demonstration, and once or twice, if James had been reasonably quiet during the lessons and made fewer interruptions than usual, he gave him lessons on how to use the cloak to baffle the bull. There was not much difficulty in getting the two of them to work; James was humiliated at having lessons with a girl, and wanted to get on far enough to join his brothers; Maria was desperately anxious not to be outstripped by an eight-year-old, especially one so cock-sure as James. Besides, she wanted the approval of her uncle, for she felt the whole question of whether she stayed at the Lodgings or went back to school depended on how well she shaped at Latin and Greek. So she wandered round the Warden's garden in the evening muttering Greek verbs to herself, and slept with grammar books under her pillow, because Hans Anderson wrote in one of his stories that if you did this you would wake in the morning knowing all the previous evening's lessons.

Mrs Clomper obviously did not care for her, so Maria tried to keep out of her way. The Warden seemed almost unaware of her presence, except at tea-time, when Maria found she was expected to pour for him, which was alarming. The heavy silver teapot and the little silver kettle over its spirit lamp were difficult to manipulate, and she was doubtful about how much cream to put into the cups. They took tea in the library so that it was only at breakfast that she saw the engraving of Jerusalem House. She could not explain why it fascinated her so much. She did not dare go into the dining-room during the daytime; whatever would she say to the maids or to Mrs Clomper, if they came in and found her there? But she used to hurry over her dressing in the morning, and hope that the housemaid would bring the hot water for washing early enough for her to be downstairs before the Warden. And then she would stand in front of the engraving, imagining herself as a tiny figure on it, walking up the tree-lined avenue. When you reached the top of the avenue there was a church on one side, and directly in front of you a small house with three upstairs windows and a vast door. Maria supposed that it must be the gatehouse. It had high walls stretching on either side of it, and to reach the main door of the house itself you would have to go through this great gate into the courtyard that lay beyond. Here, buildings surrounded you on three sides, but you walked straight on, and there, opposite the gatehouse was the main door. The house was the shape of an H, so that if she went in by the front door, which was in the middle of the bar of the H and out the other side, she would again find herself in a court surrounded by buildings on three sides. But beyond her, instead of a gatehouse, were gardens. They seemed to stretch for miles, some broken up by elaborate patterns of flower beds, others clustered with trees.

But usually, just as she was in imagination about to step out into the gardens the Warden came in, and Maria would hurriedly make for her place at the table, and turn her mind again to *amo*, and whether those decimals were right. She found mathematics torture still, though Mr Copplestone explained and explained in his good-natured but vague way, while James kicked the legs of his chair and banged his pencil on the table and said, 'Oh, come on, Maria. It's so easy.' Thomas gave her a certain amount of help, but he was so quick at solving any problem and skipped so many stages when he explained that Maria preferred to ask Joshua, who was extraordinarily patient, though not always right.

Other lessons were mostly conversation. They read Shakespeare and argued fiercely about who was to read what part, and ink usually got spilt on the tablecloth, if it had not been during the bull-fight. Or they discussed Jerusalem House. It had been decided that they should go on Friday of the week following the henhouse episode, to give the weather a sporting chance to clear. 'It will be all but June then,' said Mr Copplestone, eyeing the grey skies serenely, 'and if we can't rely on good weather in June, then when can we?'

The children were infected by his confidence. Monday, Tuesday, and Wednesday passed, cold and overcast, with a little rain, but on Thursday, at lunchtime, the clouds started moving away, and the pale sun grew stronger and stronger until by four o'clock it was shining from a clear blue sky.

'You were right about the weather, sir,' said Joshua, hanging out of the schoolroom window with ecstasy.

'Naturally,' said Mr Copplestone, offended, 'and we shall now have a fortnight of perfect summer weather.'

Maria woke already excited. She could tell by the light filtering through the heavy curtains that it was a fairly bright morning, and ran to the window to make sure. The sky was the faintest blue, and there was a light haze which promised a really hot day. It had been planned that they should row up by river to Jerusalem House, and Maria suspected that it was this part of the expedition that interested the Smiths most, though Thomas said that the tombs in the church there were very fine, and he was going to take his Epitaph Book, and also some paper and heel-ball to do brass rubbings.

'The new maid at the Lodgings has got an uncle who lives out there,' said Joshua as they sat on the wall before lunch.

'Lizzie, do you mean?' asked Maria. 'However do you know that?'

'I was talking to Laura yesterday. She let me help her clean the brass, and I told her where we were going today. She said that Lizzie from next door had an uncle with a farm out there at Long Slinfold. Jas, you can't eat brick.'

'Yes, I can. I can eat anything. I can eat wood, too. Look.' And he chewed some twig.

'I'm famished,' said Thomas, 'and it's over half an hour until lunch. Do you think we can squeeze any bread and dripping out of Cook, Jos?'

'No, she's very hot and cross preparing for a dinner party tonight. I know, because I tried to get her to let me lick a basin before we came out into the garden.'

'Jas, have you any dolly mixture?'

'No, I finished yesterday's, and I haven't bought today's yet. Let Maria go, I should think her cook has a better temper than ours.'

'I can't possibly,' said Maria, aghast.

'Why ever not?'

'Supposing Uncle Hadden or Mrs Clomper saw me?'

'What does it matter?' said Thomas. 'People must be fed; go on, you must. Take Jas with you, he always looks hungry.'

That was impossible, thought Maria; she would go through fire and water to avoid being by herself with James. 'Could Jos come with me? He can wheedle things out of people.'

'Go along, Jos,' commanded Thomas. He swung the rope

ladder over to the Warden's side of the wall. It was now lengthened and tied more securely on to the pear tree than with Mr Copplestone's piece of string. Maria scrambled down. It was rather difficult as the ladder on this side hung so close to the wall that it left no room to put one's foot in straight. She picked her way cautiously over the flower bed to the path, and then looked warily round, but the gardener was not in sight. Joshua joined her. 'Do haul up the ladder,' he urged Thomas who was almost concealed in the leaves of the pear tree, 'anyone can see it for miles.'

As they came shamefacedly into the kitchen yard Lizzie stepped out of the back door to shake a lettuce. She looked at them both with stupefaction. What could she do to her face to make it so shiny, Maria wondered. She bent down to remove some earth from her shoe and muttered, 'Go on, Jos, you say it.'

'Isn't your name Lizzie?' he began. 'You know our maid, Laura, don't you?'

Lizzie swung her bundle of lettuce uneasily and mouthed yes, without taking her eyes off him.

'She says you have an uncle who lives at Long Slinfold,' persisted Joshua.

'Yes,' breathed Lizzie.

'Do you often see him? We are going up there today by river to see Jerusalem House. Do you know it?'

Lizzie shook her head. There was a long pause. 'I've only seen my Uncle Matt but the once,' she burst out at last. 'But he be coming over for me tomorrow in the cart for to take me back to the farm for tea.'

'How very nice,' said Joshua politely. 'Hi, Maria, where are you going?' But Maria had already disappeared round the corner, and Joshua ran after her.

'Why ever did you ask her all those questions?' asked Maria, when she had recovered her breath from laughing.

'It was just a warming-up. I was coming to the bread and dripping, truly I was, only you didn't wait.'

'I couldn't wait, I knew I was going to laugh. Whatever shall we say to Thomas? I knew I would never be able to do it, I so hate asking people for things.'

'Let's go round by the road. It will take up more time.'

'No, we haven't got anything,' they called as they came up to the pear tree.

'But Lizzie's Uncle Matt is taking her over to Long Slinfold tomorrow,' called Maria, and they both started giggling again, and laughed until lunchtime.

Mrs Smith saw the party off with many instructions to everyone to behave and to sit still in the boat and to look after James. They walked out of the town to Timms' boathouse, James hurrying ahead and urging them all to walk more quickly. The river was a pale green-brown that day, and the sun seemed to soak through to one's very bones without ever feeling too hot. Maria lay in the bows and let her fingers trail through the water. Above, the bright green willows drooped down low enough for her to catch at the leaves, and on either side the meadows were bright gold with massed buttercups. Mr Copplestone and Thomas shared the rowing between them, and James was so busy looking for water-rats' holes that he hardly spoke, although he urged them once or twice to stop so that he could feed dolly mixture to a baby moorhen. Soon they had passed into territory that was new to them, beyond the farthest limits of the reaches where the Smiths used to punt. There was no other craft on the river now, and the banks seemed nearer and the cow parsley and the buttercups towered high on either side of them. The only sounds were of the oars dipping and splashing, and the cows they could not see rustling in the meadows.

'Is that it?' called Joshua. 'I think I can see some chimneys.' Mr Copplestone rested on the oars and looked over his shoulder. The boat drifted on. 'Yes, that's the house, coming into sight over the top of the rise.'

'I won't look now,' said Maria to herself, 'not until we get nearer.' And she waited until the boat slid against the bank five minutes later, and Thomas was making it fast to a tree stump. Then she turned her head, saying silently, 'Even if I die this second I shall have seen it.' But for the moment all that was to be seen was the wall. It was grey with heavy buttresses and enormously high. The fields sloped steeply up to it from the river, and inside the tops of trees showed themselves.

'Shall we be able to go into the gardens behind that wall?' asked Maria as they started the long climb up through the fields. She was fearful of being told that they could not.

'But certainly,' said Mr Copplestone, lunging at a buttercup with the umbrella he had insisted on bringing. 'And into the house too, provided the housekeeper hasn't had a fit of temperament and decided to lock all the visitors out. She is a tiresome woman.'

When they reached the top of the slope it was still a long walk round the walls. The house was concealed from them by the trees that lay within, and Maria gave little jumps from time to time in her efforts to catch a glimpse of it. After about a quarter of an hour they came to a rough road.

'This is the lane from the village,' said Mr Copplestone. 'It leads from the village to the church, which lies just outside the main entrance to the house.' They followed the lane. It ran alongside the wall, which was now broken by vast gates, leading perhaps to stable yards and coach houses. Then they saw the church, and Maria knew they had arrived. She ran the rest of the way, and there she was, standing outside the three-windowed gatehouse with, behind her, a great avenue of elms, the same avenue that she had so often imagined herself walking up. Behind the walls on either side of the gatehouse she could at last see a little of the house, a medley of roofs yellow with lichen, broken by twisted chimneys.

'The worthy Miss Hickmott is not proposing to open the doors to us until half past three,' announced Mr Copplestone, coming up behind her, 'so there is time for us to look round the church.'

Maria reluctantly followed the others into the church. It was filled with monuments to the Fitzackerley family, who had owned Jerusalem House since the beginning of time, it seemed. There were Fitzackerleys in armour, lying with their hands folded calmly and a lion at their feet, female Fitzackerleys beside them with coifs on their heads and stiffly folded dresses. There were Fitzackerleys kneeling in ruff and slashed doublet, and below them their children, eleven or twelve of them, stiff little figures identical but diminishing in size. Later Fitzackerleys in marble, larger than life size and heavily bewigged, looked as though they were striding out of coffee houses to the sound of trumpet music that cherubs were blowing below them. And the latest Fitzackerleys of all had no effigies; their epitaphs were mourned over by figures in classical draperies.

'The eighteenth-century Fitzackerleys seem to have been the goodest ones,' remarked James, studying the inscriptions, 'and the ones with the most friends: "Beloved by his many friends, esteemed and reverenced by those who served him, he was an amiable and devoted father, and an indulgent husband". Would we call Papa amiable and devoted?'

But Thomas had found a brass tablet to an even earlier Fitzackerley under a mat in the chancel and was taking a rubbing, and the others were lamenting the early deaths of the children of Humphrey, 8th Baron Fitzackerley, and nobody answered him.

At twenty-five past three Joshua said, 'Hadn't we better go, sir?' Mr Copplestone was copying an inscription into his pocket-book. Five minutes later Thomas said, 'Sir, it's

The later Fitzackerleys were in marble

half past three.' Mr Copplestone was still writing busily. 'One minute, Thomas, one minute. I cannot identify this fragment from the sixth book of the *Aeneid*. I must copy it down and look it up.' Five more minutes and he had discovered a whole sonnet. 'Most interesting. An admirer of Traherne obviously – perhaps Traherne himself. Let me commit it to paper.' The children were hovering restively at the door, eyeing the gatehouse, which had a little knot of people outside, and then turning back to Mr Copplestone to see how far he had progressed with the sonnet.

'Oh, sir,' wailed Joshua, 'They're opening the gate and everybody is going in.'

'The last line is "Here have I reached my port and ceased to mourn",' called Thomas, and they all pelted over the rough road to the grey gatehouse with its great nail-studded gates. The last visitor was stepping through the small doorway in the gates when Joshua flung himself in with a scuffle of gravel; the others following suit found themselves in the middle of a bleak-faced collection of sightseers.

'That's no way for a young gentleman to behave,' pronounced the guardian of the gate, a short white-haired man with a steely eye, 'knocking people about. Why can't you come in decent-like? You've had all afternoon to wait.'

'You mustn't shut the door,' begged Joshua, 'there's Mr Copplestone outside.' As he said this one long Copplestone leg appeared round the corner of the door which the steely-eyed man was trying to close, and then an arm.

'Isn't he like a spider monkey!' said James to the spectators.

'More like a gorilla to my mind,' said a stout woman standing beside him, 'trying to break down the place and all!'

'I'm so sorry, my good man,' said Mr Copplestone to the gatekeeper when the whole of him appeared. 'We were engrossed by your fascinating tombs. Wonderful family the Fitzackerleys.'

The gatekeeper ignored this. 'Is there any more of you to come in?' he asked.

'One girl, three boys. No, we are all here, thank you.'

The party marched forward down the stone-flagged path that led across the courtyard to the main door. 'I'm here, I'm actually inside,' whispered Maria to herself.

'That lady who may perhaps remind you of vinegar waiting for us outside the front door is the worthy Miss Hickmott,' said Mr Copplestone in a confidential way, but loud enough for Maria and Joshua to look round anxiously to see if anyone had heard. 'She is going to conduct us round.'

'Where are the Fitzackerleys?' asked Maria, 'are they away?'

'Probably skulking on the roofs with catapults,' said Thomas. 'I would if I were a young Fitzackerley.'

'The family alas has not lived here for years,' said Mr Copplestone. 'They have other seats which they seem to prefer, and so all this vast house is left to the mercy of dust sheets and Miss Hickmott.' Maria thought that this was one of the saddest things she had ever heard. All these rooms and courtyards, which must have seen so many people and heard so many feet and voices, lying empty year after year with only an occasional group of strangers peering curiously into them. The sixty seconds or so that it took to cross the courtyard was not nearly long enough for her to memorize what she saw. She had hoped to be able to have remembered every detail when she came to do her next imaginary tour on the Kips engraving, but the courtyard was crossed and she only had a blurred impression of sunbaked grey walls and mullioned windows, hundreds of them, and curious curly gables. Even James was overawed. 'What could they have used all these rooms for?' he whispered. 'Even if you had thirty children you wouldn't want all those.'

'The place was like a small town three hundred years ago,' said Mr Copplestone loudly and confidently. The rest of the party looked at him disapprovingly. Speaking, they felt, should be restricted to murmurs of admiration and amazement. 'Blacksmiths, butchers, carpenters, bricklayers, and of course all the indoor servants.' He did not have time to say more, for Miss Hickmott was coming forward to greet them, very august in purple silk, and a black satin apron embroidered with jet beads.

'Good afternoon,' she said with a thin smile. Her face was very wrinkled and yellow. 'I am going to ask you all to stay very close together and not to linger. Such a very large place, this house of ours, and we don't want anybody to get lost, do we?'

They passed through the front door, and a few steps down a passage. But instead of walking the whole length of the passage, as Maria used to do in her imaginary tour, and out into the garden the other side, they were conducted through a door in the panelling on their right. They stood in the great hall, and gazed up at its height with awe. It was very cool after the warmth outside. Fitzackerley portraits, hung high on the walls between windows far above their heads, looked down at them as though they were flies. An immensely long table ran from the slightly raised platform at the far end to the elaborately carved, ceiling-high screen through which they had just passed.

'Just think how embarrassing it would be if there were only two of you having dinner. How could you pass the salt?' said Joshua.

'Everything would be on wheels,' said James, 'like that cheese coaster Papa showed us.'

Miss Hickmott rapidly named the subjects of the portraits in the dim heights, gave a quelling look to the party, and said, 'And now we proceed to the Great Staircase.' The party trailed meekly after her towards a door at the far end of the hall.

'But it's so small,' complained James, 'it's not great.' Indeed, the staircase was a surprise in so large a house; carpetless and tucked away in a corner, it was hardly the sort of staircase that Maria had imagined for herself, where she could sweep slowly down with a silken rustle. This staircase in three flights, where one would have to turn three corners, was useless if one wanted to make a stately entrance. The children dragged behind the rest of the party. At the top of the stairs they peered into a long gallery that opened off the landing, but Miss Hickmott said freezingly, 'We shall all have an opportunity to inspect Lady Margaret's Gallery on the return journey,' and she swept them off through a long succession of rooms that lay on the other side of the landing, each one opening off another. The furniture lay cased in white covers, and all colour and life seemed to have left the rooms, except where the sun, shining through the coats of arms in the glass of the few windows that had no blinds over them, made red and blue patterns on the floor. Maria tried to linger behind the others, but Miss Hickmott always hounded her on. She was finding Mr Copplestone's party a great trial; Mr Copplestone himself was darting from picture to picture, taking elaborate notes, Thomas and Joshua were peeping out of the windows or loitering in front of portraits of juvenile Fitzackerleys, and James was always ahead trying to see what lay round the next corner.

'He didn't ought to have brought children on a serious visit like this,' said the stout woman who had already complained about them, to her husband, 'not that our Emmy and Alfred wouldn't have behaved a sight better than these.' 'Skipping about and looking at all the pictures like that,' said the husband, who had heavy sandy whiskers and a large gold watch chain.

There were bedrooms with beds reaching from ceiling to floor, hung with curtains of faded blue and green and red. Miss Hickmott would jerk up the yellow blinds for an instant and let in a flood of sunshine that made everybody blink, and then slam them down again.

'I have always wanted to know,' said Mr Copplestone pleasantly, 'if you make up the beds with blankets and sheets to achieve that comfortable look, and if so how often you have to change them. Might one be permitted to ask?'

'That is a question that only concerns the linen room,' said Miss Hickmott frostily.

'What a question to ask,' whispered the fat woman loudly, 'and him a clergyman too! Prying into things that aren't his business!'

'Where could they have kept their clothes, do you think?' Joshua asked Maria, 'there's nothing in these bedrooms but beds and chairs.'

By this time Maria was too cross and disappointed to speak. It was far better wandering round the house in imagination than walking briskly after the housekeeper and being told not to loiter every time she wanted to look. They were now retracing their steps through the line of rooms, and at last arrived back where they had started, at the top of the Great Staircase.

'Before we descend the staircase again, we will take a look at Lady Margaret's Gallery,' Miss Hickmott was saying to her docile flock, and she led them into the immensely long room into which the children had already peered. It was lit with windows the entire length of one side and at the far end. James was thoroughly bored by this time and was working out a long sum to calculate how many hours a year one person could spend in each room if there were two hundred and fifty, as Miss Hickmott said there were. Thomas and Joshua just stood staring out of the nearest window at the garden below. Miss Hickmott catalogued the portraits, and Maria obediently followed her eye, feeling that she ought to try very hard to concentrate as this was the last room. After all, had she not wanted to go to Jerusalem House more than anywhere else in the world?

'Fitzackerley . . . Fitzackerley . . .' droned Miss Hickmott, passing rapidly down the line of faded portraits that hung there. All the men seemed to be called Richard or Humphrey, and as their names were painted on the frames anyway, there seemed little point in calling them out. 'Stephen Fitzackerley, Deborah Fitzackerley,' she finished, 'Children of the ninth baron.' At the word 'children' the Smiths turned round and looked.

'Oh, but they're only babies,' said James glumly, after peering at the picture, which showed a round-faced small girl with a cockatoo on her arm and a solemn little boy beside her. 'There's a drawing of a boy over there which is more interesting.' He waved vaguely towards the bottom of the gallery. Maria and the Smiths moved down the room to look at it. It was hung high up in a dark corner, and was difficult to see properly but they could make out the head and shoulders of a boy with a curiously beaky nose and a high forehead. It was drawn in what looked like black chalk on blue paper.

'He looks rather nice,' said Thomas. 'I'm sure he would lurk around with a catapult and shy stones at Miss Hickmott and her party.'

'Do you think he's a Fitzackerley?' Maria asked.

'Sure to be, otherwise why is he here at all.'

'He might have been a little cousin, or a godchild. After all, there weren't photographs, and people would have to have had portraits made instead. You don't expect every photograph in a house to be of the family.'

'Don't be so argumentative, Maria, you must have caught it from so many lessons with James,' said Thomas. 'If you want extra proof, just look at that nose and forehead. That's Fitzackerley all right, all the other portraits in the room have got it, only it seems to come out more in a drawing.'

' "An Unknown Boy",' read out James from tiny letters painted on the frame, 'I can see better than any of you and I'm the smallest. I've got wonderful eyes.'

'We could have seen it if we had wanted to,' said Thomas cuttingly. 'But we were concentrating on the drawing instead. The label should read "An Unknown Fitzackerley"; I've a good mind to tell Miss Hickmott so.'

'I bet you won't,' said James, revolving on his heels, 'I've got wonderful eyes, better than anybody in the world.'

Thomas was just reaching out to shake him when there was a rustle of silk, and Miss Hickmott, grim and black, advanced down the gallery towards them. 'Young people,' she said, 'has no one ever taught you to do as you are told, and not to keep your elders waiting?'

As they hustled downstairs, Maria and Joshua with burning cheeks, Thomas and James thoroughly resentful, James poked Thomas. 'Go on,' he whispered, 'ask her.'

They were nearly at the bottom of the stairs now. Thomas, giving James a ferocious look, hurried to catch up the housekeeper. 'Oh, Miss Hickmott,' he said, clearing his throat, a sign by which the children knew he was nervous, 'that drawing that we were looking at was called "An Unknown Boy", but it is a Fitzackerley boy, isn't it?'

'Young gentleman,' said Miss Hickmott, folding her lips primly, and speaking straight into the void in front of her, 'if one of our portraits is labelled "unknown", you can be sure that it is unknown. We do not go in for untruths here.'

'All the same, it *is* a Fitzackerley,' muttered Thomas furiously as he fell back. 'And I bet it would be quite easy to find out who he was.'

'Why not, indeed,' said Mr Copplestone, who was leaning languidly against the great table in the hall, pointing the toe of his shoe and smiling down at its brilliant polish. 'It would make a good subject for a learned paper. Miss Hickmott!' He wandered slowly over to the housekeeper who was gathering up her brood by the force of her eye alone. 'Our young friends here have the ambition to do a little research into the identity of a portrait. Would they be given facilities to do so, do you think?'

The Smiths stood horrified at this final baiting of the enemy. 'Most certainly not,' snapped Miss Hickmott, 'I consider the suggestion the grossest impertinence.'

'Ah,' mourned Mr Copplestone, 'the pursuit of truth was never an easy task.'

Ignoring him, Miss Hickmott stalked forward, her party shuffling behind her. 'And now we come to the gardens, said to be the most magnificent seventeenth-century gardens in the whole of England. Laid out by the ninth Lord Fitzackerley between 1631 and 1640, they have never been altered.'

'That is only because the family lacked the money to do anything about it later on,' said Mr Copplestone in a cheerful whisper. 'You would never catch an eighteenth-century landowner putting up with this old-fashioned sort of thing if he had the means to do anything about it.' Then ignoring the indignant looks of the other members of the party, he addressed himself again to Miss Hickmott. 'I hope we may be allowed to promenade round these delightful gardens before the curfew tolls.'

'Ten minutes are allowed for the inspection of the gardens,' said Miss Hickmott, turning her back on him. 'Jerusalem House closes to the public at half past four, and I must ask everybody without fail to assemble here at that time, and not to go out of sight of the house.' She stood back to allow them to straggle through the passage and out into the sun beyond. They stood blinking in the sudden dazzle of light, in a grassy court surrounded on three sides by the house.

'I must say it's been a pretty fearful afternoon,' said Thomas, wandering slowly forward across the grass, 'what with that Miss Hickmott and Mr Copplestone and all. Now for heaven's sake, don't let's cross her again. She's expecting us to misbehave, so we'll behave like angels.' They were standing now on a terrace of grass overlooking a garden where miniature box hedges curved in dark lines to form a vast pattern of scrolls and whirls. They went down stone steps into this garden and walked slowly down the gravel path that ran through it. Joshua kept turning round to make sure the house was still in sight. 'Mr Copplestone's sitting down and drawing things in his note-book,' he said anxiously. 'I'm sure the housekeeper won't like that.'

'Well, let him deal with her then,' said Thomas, 'at least we're not involved. Nobody could possibly object to what we're doing. How ugly this garden is, all those horrid little hedges and not a single flower. I don't see anything magnificent about it.'

The garden of box hedges finished, and they stood at the top of more stone steps looking down at a garden of yew bushes, clipped into fantastic shapes, some animal, some geometric.

'We've got time to go down here,' said Thomas.

'Will we be within sight of the house?' asked Joshua nervously.

'Look back and see for yourself. I can see hundreds of chimneys and the roof, but perhaps your eye can't reach so far.' Thomas strolled nonchalantly on.

'It all depends what "within sight of" means,' said Joshua. 'Does it mean that we ought to be able to see the house, or that somebody in the house ought to be able to see us?'

'Joshua, you'll drive me mad. Don't fuss, man, you're as bad as Mamma.'

But they had come to the end of this garden now, and an impenetrable yew hedge rose up in front of them. 'There are kitchen gardens and orchards and things through there,' said Maria. 'I remember from the engraving in Uncle

Hadden's dining-room. And when you had gone through all those you would come to the wall we walked round to get here.'

'Anyway, we couldn't go any farther,' said Thomas, consulting his watch, 'we've taken four and a half minutes to get here, it will be four and a half minutes back, and we'll have a minute in hand to glare at Miss Hickmott and collect the Streak.'

When they reached Mr Copplestone they found him trying to draw the elaborate curves of the box hedges in his note-book. 'It is very unfortunate that I seem to have reached the end of my note-book,' he said without looking up, 'but I am drawing it over the copy of the Traherne sonnet. I do not think either will suffer.'

'We've only got a minute more, sir,' said Thomas. But Miss Hickmott, remembering the trouble she had had with this party the whole afternoon, came over with a determined expression.

'Aha, Miss Hickmott! What do you find here but a spy making secret charts!' Mr Copplestone clapped his note-book shut, stood up, and wagged his finger at her. 'Be watchful, be vigilant, otherwise you will wake in the middle of one night and find yourself being blown through the roof by the gunpowder I have planted in the cellars.'

The party straggled out through the house into the courtyard, under the gatehouse where the man with the steely eye stood watchfully, in case one of the sightseers was trying to smuggle out a portrait underneath his overcoat. He clanged the door shut behind them, and Jerusalem House once more became impenetrable to the outside world.

CHAPTER FIVE

Truth or Dare?

THE next day was Saturday, and though she had so far experienced only one Maria had decided that for her, Saturday was the worst day of the week. Monday to Friday was a planned time-table of lessons and homework, and Sunday followed its own pattern – she took all her meals with the Warden, for one thing, and sat with him in the library in the evening. But Saturday was dreary. She was not supposed to go farther than the Smiths' house without being accompanied by some adult, and the Smiths were usually occupied with their father, who made a practice of devoting most of his Saturday afternoons to his sons. The library was at her disposal, so she used to wander round there for a little, pulling out books and then feeling bored with them before she had read a page. But all the time she would be rather afraid in case the Warden came in. Would he remember that he had told her to use the library? The other day, indeed, he had come in with the Bishop while she was sitting on top of the library ladder reading, and she had not known whether to stay up there or come down to say how-do-you-do. However, she did not feel like the library today. She wandered round the garden and eyed such windows of the Smiths' house as she could see through the trees. A spray of water caught her smartly on one cheek. She clapped her hand there and looked angrily in the direction from which it had come. Thomas's head was visible on the other side of the wall. He guffawed, and then heaved himself up, first elbows and then knees, until he was sitting there with his legs dangling.

'That was the garden syringe. It's very powerful and shoots water a tremendous distance. I want to try it on birds.'

'What were you standing on?'

'The henhouse.'

'However did you dare?'

'My weight couldn't possibly break it. Anyhow, I had to. The last person to come down from the wall has to tie up the ladder in the pear tree and jump down, and it's the job of the first person up to untie it. Aren't you glad it's Saturday?'

Maria hesitated. 'I think Saturdays are rather dull. Do you like them specially?'

'No lessons,' said Thomas confidentially. 'Doing Virgil and Cicero with Papa is rather a strain, you know. Mr Ledgard is all right, he knows exactly what he has taught us and what things we ought to know, but Papa thinks we are much more advanced than we are, and gets very impatient. I forgot to tell you: Mamma thinks Jas has got scarlet fever, we shall probably all get it now.'

Staying in bed and being nursed by Mrs Clomper! Maria's heart sank. 'Scarlet fever! How dreadful! He seemed all right yesterday.'

'He's got a bit of a sore throat today and a temperature and Mamma thinks she can see a rash coming. The doctor just says "Wait and see, my little man". But Jas swears he hasn't got scarlet fever; he seems very confident.'

'Poor Jas.'

'Poor Nurse! She's having a terrible time trying to keep him in bed. It's going to be a dismal week-end. Mamma's in a state, and Papa's said he's got no time for any of us and has shut himself in the study.'

'"I am aweary, weary, would that I were dead", said Maria, remembering poetry readings with her governess.

'What's that?'

'It's from a poem by Tennyson. About a girl waiting for her lover.'

The other day he had come in with the Bishop

'Very apt, considering it's such a foolish subject. What *are* we going to do today? You suggest something.'

This was flattering, but all the same alarming. It was hardly likely that Maria, whose only experience of games had been with a brood of girls, could think of anything that would satisfy Thomas. There was a scrabbling from the other side of the wall. 'Jos is going to come up now,' said Thomas, and shifted to make room for him. 'Look at that blackbird on the lawn. I'm going to try to hit it with this squirt.' The water landed short of the blackbird, who gave a warning 'kerk-kerk-kerk' and flew off. Joshua heaved himself up on his elbows.

'Jos,' commanded Thomas, 'think of some way of occupying this dreary afternoon.'

'Well, not Truth or Dare anyway.'

'That's a brilliant idea,' said Thomas, giving him a heavy slap on the back. 'We haven't played it for months, and Maria will provide an interesting new element.'

'But I said *not* Truth or Dare,' wailed Joshua. 'It's a hateful game.'

'It isn't, if you play it properly. And I'll let you down lightly.'

'What is it about?' Maria asked.

'We take it in turns to ask each other "truth or dare?" If you answer "truth" the other person can ask you whatever question he likes, and you've got to tell the truth. If you say "dare" he can dare you to do something.'

'Supposing you won't do it?'

'But you must. Unless the others agree that it's impossible. And you're not allowed to say "truth" more than twice, because there's a limit to the things one wants to know about people. In fact, I know all there is to be known about old Joshua. Cheer up, Jos, at least James isn't here, he's the one who sets awful dares.'

'Yours aren't much better.'

'I tell you what, you can start,' offered Thomas, 'and none of your milk and water dares. There must be some difficulty in them.'

'Very well, then. Maria, "truth or dare?"'

'Dare.' Maria calculated that it would be wiser to save her truths for Thomas. Joshua looked up at the sky vacantly. It was obvious that he had not an idea about what to ask. After a long pause during which Thomas sighed and kicked his heels with impatience, he said, 'Oh, jump off this wall then.' With the rope ladder to get her to the top of the wall, Maria managed it without any difficulty, and jumped down back into the Warden's garden, into the compost heap farther along.

'Now it's my turn to ask,' said Thomas. 'Jos, I suppose you'll have "truth" as usual?'

'Yes,' said Joshua. He always hoped that by the time he had to start on the dares, the others would have become tired of the game.

'Very well. What do you think of Maria then? Do you like her coming over for lessons?'

Joshua and Maria looked at each other furtively. There was a long pause, and Maria began to blush. 'Well, I do like her. But if she didn't come to lessons we wouldn't have to have some of ours with Papa. Thos, that was a horrible question.'

'There's no sense in asking questions unless they're embarrassing ones. Now, Maria, I'm going to "truth or dare" you.'

'Dare,' said Maria hastily, terrified in case Thomas would ask her what she thought of his father.

'Go up to the Warden's study window then, and stay there looking while I count ten.'

Maria was appalled. 'You can't make me do anything so awful. He may be there.'

'If I didn't think he was there I wouldn't have suggested it.'

'What happens if I don't go?'

'You are branded as a coward for the rest of your days and not spoken to by us. And if Papa or Mr Copplestone or anybody asks us why we aren't speaking to you we would have to tell them the truth. It's a perfectly simple dare, after all. You have been let off very lightly.'

Joshua watched her with sympathy as she slunk off. She made a wide detour to avoid being seen from the study while she was advancing on it, and then hovered ten yards away on the lawn.

'Go on, closer,' called Thomas faintly from the wall. Maria took four desperate strides, which brought her to the edge of the flower bed below the window. She was standing towards one side, and at first could see nothing except her own reflection on the pane. Then she made out the tall black figure of her uncle standing and reaching up for a book. She counted twelve for good measure, and then darted off, feeling her heart pounding as though it would burst out of her.

'A very short ten,' commented Thomas, 'but we shall have to let it pass. Now it's your turn, Maria. Be bold, be brave, be resolute.'

But Maria was panting so hard with fear and relief at having escaped being seen by her uncle that she could hardly speak. 'To save your breath,' added Thomas, 'I'll take a dare.'

'All right then,' said Maria grimly, 'I dare you to go to Jerusalem House and break in.'

There was an astonished silence. 'That's an impossible dare,' said Joshua firmly.

'No, it's not,' Thomas said unexpectedly. 'It's rather a good one, if you give me time to work out the details. Only, to pay you back, Maria, for setting me something you thought I couldn't possibly do, you can come too. And Joshua can come as a referee, to judge whether I carry it out properly. Only he won't, of course. He'll be in such a dither that I'll only have to set a foot in the park for him to say that I've done it and we'd better go home now. Actually it's rather a good way of getting away from the sickroom atmosphere that the house is smothered in today.'

'Thos, you're only teasing, aren't you?' Joshua asked anxiously. 'You aren't really meaning to go?'

'Indeed I am. Unless Maria wants to take back her dare.'

'I'll take it back if you want me to.' Maria hoped hard that he would want her to do so.

'Of course I wouldn't ask you to. You must do it of your own free will.'

'There's no way of getting there,' said Joshua triumphantly. 'Timms would never let us take a boat out by ourselves. And unless you're proposing to walk I don't see how else we can do it.'

'Lizzie's Uncle Matt,' said Maria, hardly knowing what she was saying. Joshua remembered quickly enough. 'Of course we can't.'

'What are you two talking about?' said Thomas impatiently. 'Will someone kindly explain?'

'Our kitchen-maid Lizzie,' Maria told him reluctantly. 'Her Uncle Matt was coming over today by cart to take her back to Long Slinfold with him. She told us yesterday.'

'And we could go with her, you mean. A good idea,' said Thomas briskly. 'Action!' and he gave a colossal leap off the wall into the flower bed; Maria anxiously smoothed over his footprints. 'To Lizzie, forward march. You can stay on the wall if you like, Jos.'

They both hung around outside the kitchen door. 'It's no good,' said Thomas, 'I can see she's not in the kitchen, only your cook is there. You'll have to scout round the house, Maria, and tell her to come out.' Maria eventually discovered her polishing knives in the pantry. 'Could you possibly come to the door leading to the garden?' she asked in a whisper. 'It's rather important.' Lizzie dropped her knives and rubbed her hands nervously on her apron. She looked still more nervous when Thomas questioned her about her Uncle Matt, but they managed to get out of her that he was going to meet her by St Giles Church at half past two that afternoon after she had washed up from luncheon, and yes, she thought he would take them with him to Long Slinfold.

'You won't tell anyone, will you?' begged Maria. Lizzie shook her head dumbly and hurried in. Maria and Thomas went back to the wall.

'You're really meaning to go?' said Joshua after they had told him of their success with Lizzie.

'I certainly am,' said Thomas. 'We'll meet you at a quarter past two outside the college, Maria, and presumably you will have thought up an excuse for Mrs Clomper. We'll deal with Mamma, which will be far more difficult; she asks so many questions.'

Maria duly explained to Mrs Clomper that she had been asked out for a walk by the Smiths, and would it be all right if she did not take her usual Saturday afternoon walk with her that day. To her surprise Mrs Clomper accepted this and asked no awkward questions about whether there was to be a grown-up in charge of the party. No doubt she assumed, Maria thought guiltily, that the professor himself was taking them. As she waited nervously outside the college Professor Smith strode past in his top-hat. 'Aha, Maria,' he called out, 'going out on an epitaph-hunting expedition with the boys, I hear. I'm sorry we cannot produce James to complete the party, but his mother thinks he is going to develop scarlet fever. James swears he is not – he believes evidently in the superiority of mind over matter. I have great faith in James's determination, great faith.'

As he marched on down the street, Thomas and Joshua emerged from the house. 'I can tell you that this scarlet fever is an act of God,' said Thomas, 'we couldn't possibly have taken James with us. Joshua is bad enough, he has cold feet already.'

Joshua dragged the toe of a boot over the cobbles. 'So many things can go wrong. And how can we get into the house even if we get there?'

'We are going to look at the church first,' Thomas told him. 'The house can wait. We told Papa we were going on an epitaph-hunting expedition, and epitaphs we must hunt.'

'But I am sure he thinks we are only going round the corner to St Cross churchyard,' said Joshua mournfully.

'Well, we can't be responsible for his illusions,' said Thomas grandly. 'Come along.'

Lizzie was already sitting in the cart with Uncle Matt when they reached St Giles Church. Uncle Matt was a very red man with hair that sprouted out of his ears. He nodded to the children and waved his whip at the back of the cart. They clambered up and sat in a row along the seat, their backs to Lizzie and her uncle. 'What will we do if anybody sees us?' whispered Joshua.

'Let them see us!'

'They'll tell Mamma; we're so conspicuous perched up here.'

'You'll make yourself far more conspicuous if you start behaving like an ostrich. Sit up and look indifferent, you ass.'

Joshua stopped trying to hide his head behind Maria, and sat on the edge of the seat looking extremely nervous. Every few minutes he asked Thomas what the time was. Lizzie seemed overpowered both by the presence of her uncle and of the children, and did not say a word. Her uncle occasionally tossed out an item of information to her without taking his eyes off the road. 'Your Aunt May had three of her hens took by a fox.' 'We buried the rector's lady last week.' 'Hay's early this year.'

The plump quarters of the flea-bitten grey mare jogged up and down as she trotted briskly northwards. It seemed a very long way to Long Slinfold by road. Maria felt almost as nervous as Joshua, but knowing how much it would irritate Thomas, she tried to hide it. The obstacles to this expedition were far bigger than those on the escape to Oxford. (1) Getting to Long Slinfold without being stopped. (2) Finding Jerusalem House. (3) Getting into the house. (4) Getting out. (5) Coming home safely. And of these numbers 3, 4, and 5, seemed highly dangerous. However, she thought, it must be miles and miles away yet.

The roads were white and rutted and puffs of dust flew from under the mare's hooves. Now that they were on the Long Slinfold road they met very little traffic. Once a tall gig overtook them ('Dr Slim,' said Uncle Matt. 'Mrs Marsh must be took bad again') and once they passed a carriage with a liveried coachman and footman. This, Uncle Matt remarked, was Lady Glosters out visiting. The sun was very hot in a clear pale-blue sky. In some of the fields they were bringing in the hay, and wisps hung on the hedges to show where carts had already passed. Invisible larks shrilled above their heads. 'What a dull county Oxford is,' said Joshua crossly. But gradually the bare flat fields merged into more wooded country, and elm trees crowded in on the road. 'Not far now,' said Uncle Matt without turning his head. As they turned a corner a lodge appeared, nearly smothered in trees, and then as the cart neared it they saw enormous iron gates flanked by columns on which a stone lion pranced.

'This is the avenue that leads up to the house,' said Maria with excitement, recognizing the lodge that appeared on the Kips engraving.

'Hadn't we better go on till we reach the road that goes past the church?' objected Joshua. 'You remember Mr Copplestone said it was the regular road from the church to the village.' But Uncle Matt was stopping the cart. 'If it's Jerusalem House you want, young gentlemen, you had better

It seemed a very long way to Long Slinfold by road

get down here.' They jumped down. In the garden in front of the lodge a man in his shirt sleeves had stopped staking up his peas to look at them.

'Thomas, we can't possibly get inside,' said Joshua, pulling at his sleeve. 'Anyway, that man's looking at us. Come on, do let's go on into the village and find the road there.' But the man in the shirt sleeves straightened himself and waved. 'Well, Matt, and who's that you've got with you?'

'Young lady and young gentlemen who want to have a look at the house. That all right?'

The lodgekeeper looked doubtfully at the three of them. 'Oh, I dare say. But you keep out of those woods, young sirs, and don't you go racketing around. Just up to the top of the avenue and have a look at the house, see.'

'We'll be coming back this way at half past five,' said Uncle Matt, 'or you can come along to Gandershatch Farm and meet us there. Anyone'll tell you the way.' He flicked his whip and called to the mare, and the cart clip-clopped into the distance.

'Half past five!' Maria was horrified. 'It took us an hour to get here so we won't be back till half past six, and they will be expecting me for tea!'

Thomas shrugged. 'There's no way of getting back now; we shall just have to make the best of it and enjoy ourselves while we can.'

The lodgekeeper pulled open one of the gates for them. 'It's about half a mile up the avenue. And mind, no tomfooling when you get there!'

'What tomfooling does he expect?' muttered Thomas. 'Those walls round the house would stand up to an army, let alone the three of us.'

'But we don't even know where this road is taking us,' lamented Joshua, kicking despondently at a stone.

'Yes, we do,' said his brother impatiently. 'It brings us

out by the church and the gatehouse. Surely you remember seeing an avenue from there?'

'What are we going to do when we get there?'

'Have a look at the church, of course, nobody can stop us doing that. After all, it's the village church, even though it is a long way from the village. Anybody has a right to go into it.' Thomas strode on up the avenue, Maria behind him giving anxious sidelong looks at Joshua. She was afraid he was going to sit down and refuse to go farther. 'It will be all right, Jos, really,' she assured him. 'After all, we can always say the man at the lodge told us we could come.' Thomas looked over his shoulder. 'Now, don't start worrying about Joshua, Maria, he'll be all right. Females never can be single-minded; they always have to worry about everything.'

They marched on in silence. The grey mass that had been visible in front of them, at the distant mouth of the tunnel of great elms under which they were walking, gradually became recognizable as the gatehouse. Maria ran to catch up Thomas. 'Are you really going to try to get in?'

'What I thought we could do was to walk round the walls in the direction of the river, the way we came yesterday, and see if we can find any gates. But the tombs first, because of what we told Papa we were going to do.'

They emerged from the dappled shadows of the avenue and stood in the full sunlight. Opposite them was the enormous length of wall which held within it the small township of Jerusalem House and all its gardens. The church stood to their left, a little way from the walls. Thomas pushed open the door. As they stood in the dim light of the church they realized by the movements from the chancel that somebody else was already there. A woman smiling brightly rustled down the nave towards them, holding some irises. 'Have you come to see our beautiful church? How very nice. You look round and I'll tell you anything you want to know when I have finished arranging these flowers.'

After that all desire to look round left them, and they stood glumly among the Fitzackerley tombs. Maria peered up at the tablets on the walls. 'There's one to a girl who died when she was ten,' she whispered, 'called Deborah.'

'There was a picture of a girl called Deborah in that gallery yesterday,' said Thomas. 'She had a cockatoo on her arm. It was about the only interesting picture in the whole grisly collection – except for that drawing.'

'Perhaps it was the same girl.' Maria said. 'This one died in 1652, daughter of the ninth Lord Fitzackerley.'

'I don't see why it should be.' Joshua was in an argumentative mood. 'There were probably masses of Deborahs, as many as the Richards and Humphreys.'

'Very well then,' said Thomas, 'we'll settle it by asking that woman.'

'Oh, no, Thos,' begged Joshua, coming quickly to his normal frame of mind. 'I expect Maria was right.'

But Thomas had already strode off. 'Excuse me,' they could hear him saying politely, 'but are there many people called Deborah buried here? My brother wants to know.'

'Oh, help!' muttered Joshua, 'let's get out, quickly.'

Thomas found them in the churchyard. 'Why ever did you go rushing off like that? She says that it is the only Deborah she has heard of in the family, and what a beautiful Bible name it is, isn't it.'

At that moment they heard movements in the porch and started examining the gravestones with great attention, though the grass was so long that it was difficult to see the inscriptions on them. The woman went down the path, and paused with her hand on the gate. 'You are serious-minded little people, aren't you?' she said. 'I'm afraid you won't find those gravestones very interesting, though.'

'Oh, yes we do, thank you very much,' said Joshua desperately; he could see by Thomas's face what he thought of being called 'a little person'. 'We like to see whether husbands and wives ever die on the same day, and if there are any children. It's very kind of you to have helped us. Thomas, look, I think there are some quite interesting ones over here.' And all three of them bent down and pushed grass away from the stones as eagerly as though they were hunting for treasure.

'She's gone now,' whispered Maria, stealing a glance at the grey bustle retreating down the lane to the village.

'Come on, make for the wall,' ordered Thomas. 'We want to get out of sight of the avenue as soon as possible, only don't run, because anyone who saw us would be suspicious.' But they waited until she was out of sight before they started down the lane in her wake. They hurried past the massive gates of the stable yards that looked as though they had not been opened for centuries. At last they reached the point where they could leave the road and follow the wall through fields.

'I don't know how far we have got to walk to find a gate,' said Thomas. 'And we haven't such a great deal of time.'

They plodded on, but the wall was blank and impenetrable. 'Look,' called Maria, who had almost given up hope, 'there seems to be a sort of dip in the wall just there. I think perhaps it's a gate.' She broke into a run. It was a gate, a faded blue one, blistered by the sun. Thomas pushed it. It opened with difficulty because the grass was so long inside, and they all squeezed through the crack and shut it again. They were in an old apple orchard, where the trees grew tall and gnarled.

'We're trespassing,' moaned Joshua. 'Maria, hasn't he gone far enough for your dare?'

'Now, look here, Jos,' said Thomas, 'it's time you stopped behaving like a peahen in distress. Either you wait outside the wall until we come back, or you stay with us and behave sensibly. Which is it to be?'

'Of course I'll come with you. It would be dreadful waiting alone.'

'Well, cooperate then.'

'How far are you going?'

'Into the gardens where we were yesterday, if we can find our way back into them.'

'If anybody comes we can always say that the gate was open and that we didn't realize we were trespassing,' said Maria.

'Yes, Jos, and the worst we can get is a few minutes of somebody's anger.'

'But I hate anger.'

'Never mind, you probably won't even get that.'

'They'll be plenty of it at home,' said Joshua gloomily.

They rustled through the orchard grass, pausing now and then to listen for gardeners. But the only sound to be heard was the soothing rippling of a distant wood-pigeon. Maria touched Thomas's arm and pointed. Ahead of them lay another blue gate; the orchard grass grew high against it and the latch and hinges were red with rust. Even Thomas hesitated before he opened it. It was like entering a lost world. They stepped out into the shade of immensely high hedges. 'It must be that garden where the yew bushes are,' whispered Maria. 'There was an enormous hedge at the bottom of it. If we walk down to that opening there I think we'll find ourselves in the garden.'

The gravel of the path sounded very noisy, and it occurred to Maria that while you could fairly easily pretend that you thought the orchard was a field and that you were looking for a way through, the same could not be said to someone who found you in the middle of an elaborately laid out garden.

'The best thing to say if we get caught,' whispered Thomas, as if he had guessed her thoughts, 'is that we were so very anxious to see the gardens of Jerusalem House. That's true enough, and grown-ups always like one to be keen.'

'Miss Hickmott doesn't,' Joshua said dismally.

However, reassured by having an answer ready to offer, even though it was not a very good one, they crept forward. Then suddenly they were out of the shadows cast by the yew hedges, and blinking in the sunlight of the garden of the fancifully clipped yew bushes. Thomas led them up the broad gravel path, up the steps at the end, and there was Jerusalem House about a hundred yards away from them, its windows veiled by yellow blinds. They all felt that the eyes of scores of watchers in the house must be fastened on them, and darted down the steps again.

'Well, there you are, you've done it now,' whispered Joshua anxiously. 'Shall we go back now?'

'What did you say in your dare, Maria?' Thomas asked.

'I can't remember. Anyway, I'm sure you've carried it out.' But Thomas had been made bold by their success. 'I think you said, "break into the house".'

'This is breaking into the house. We broke through a gate into the garden. We can't possibly get any farther, Miss Hickmott will have bolted every door and window – besides, just think how frightful it would be to meet her.'

'We'll split the difference,' said Thomas obstinately. 'I'll go to the top of the next lot of steps – the ones that lead up from the garden with the silly box hedges on to the terrace.'

'Oh, no, Thos,' wailed Joshua, 'you're bound to be seen.'

'No one can see me. There's a blind in every single window. You stay safe down here. I won't be long.'

Maria watched him go a few paces, and then ran after him. It would be less agonizing to take part in the danger than just to look on. They walked swiftly up the path, hesitated for an instant at the bottom of the steps, and then ran up them two at a time. It was just as they reached the top that a sound broke the stillness of the house and garden, the sound of bolts being drawn on the door facing them. Thomas took the whole flight of steps in one jump and Maria followed him. They crouched on the gravel with thudding hearts, and listened. The door was opened, and after a few seconds was banged shut. But had anybody come out? As she knelt at the bottom of the steps with her face only a foot or so from the parapet, Maria noticed what seemed to be writing carved on the stone. Somebody had carved his initials there, S. St G. F. And there was something written above. Maria craned an inch or two nearer to read it, and then jumped back in sudden fright. The inscription, cut deep into the stone, read, 'Begone, ye foul traitors', and for the moment it seemed as though it was meant for them. Thomas, behind her, poked her in the ankle reprovingly, and they crouched there very still for a few more minutes. Then, as no further sound came from above, Thomas crawled up to her ear, and muttered, 'I think whoever it was is safely behind the door again. But we'd better keep as low as we can on the way back.'

'Look,' Maria whispered, and showed him the writing. Thomas examined it, and then pointed to a date under the initial. '20 July 1654,' he whispered. 'It's funny to think people carved their names then.'

They ran back across the garden of box hedges, bent almost double, and when they came to the top of the next flight of steps they found Joshua crouching at the bottom.

He looked up at them. 'Oh, dear, it was awful. I went to the top of these steps to look for you and you were running up the steps on to the terrace.'

'Worse things happened than that,' Thomas told him. 'Somebody opened the door. But then they shut it again, and here we are, perfectly sound in wind and limb.'

'Not in wind,' said Maria. 'It's dreadful running doubled up, and it couldn't have made any difference to whether people could see us.' She felt very elated after the danger they had faced and escaped. 'We saw a very interesting inscription. It was written in 1654, and said, "Begone, ye foul traitors." Do you think it was a Royalist trying to insult Roundheads, Thomas?'

'More likely somebody's joke,' said Thomas dampingly. 'It's the sort of thing I would like to do, only the trouble is that you can't be around all the time to see people fall into the trap.'

'S. St G. F.,' Maria went on. 'The F might be for Fitzackerley.' By this time they were in the orchard, and she hurried through the long grass to catch up Thomas who was a few paces ahead. 'Thomas, the F might easily be for Fitzackerley, mightn't it? Stephen Fitzackerley, that boy in the picture with the girl holding a cockatoo. Yes, it fits it.' She was growing excited. 'That girl was called Deborah, and we saw in the church that she died in 1652 – if it was the same girl – and if that boy in the picture is the brother of the girl buried in the church then he easily might have carved that inscription in 1654.'

'Most ingenious and most unlikely and far too many ifs,' said Thomas in his maddening way, 'and *if* we don't want to miss Uncle Matt and the cart and spend all night in the avenue, we had better hurry, I think.'

This made Joshua walk at a furious rate, and run when he had enough breath, and he paid no attention to Thomas, who shouted after him when they reached the avenue, that there was plenty of time now. They waited in silence outside the lodge; they could see the lodgekeeper inside, taking his tea, surrounded by his family; and at twenty-five to six the cart rounded the corner. Uncle Matt raised his whip to them in salute without a flicker of expression, and Lizzie just stared very hard at her boots. Not a word was said on the journey back. Uncle Matt put them down at St Giles Church, and while Lizzie stayed behind to say good-bye the other three hurried off.

'There's James at the bedroom window,' said Joshua as they walked down Canterbury Lane. Maria looked up and saw a figure muffled in a shawl standing at the second floor window from which the Smiths commanded such a magnificent view of the comings and goings in the road below. The figure beat on the window and its mouth moved in words they could not hear. They stood and looked at him. Thomas put his hand to his ear and raised his eyebrows. The window was flung up and James leaned out. 'Wherever have you been? Mamma's in such a state. There's going to be a great row.' James then disappeared with great suddenness; Nurse came over and banged down the window.

'There's going to be a great row there too,' observed Thomas with satisfaction.

CHAPTER SIX

War and Peace

THERE was indeed a great row. Professor Smith opened the front door and looked them up and down for a full half minute before he began on them.

'So there you are, you wretched miscreants. Do you realize what you have exposed me to, what untold harm you have done to the cause of learning? Your mamma sufficiently overwrought by James's scarlet fever, and on top of that you choose to disappear for hours on end! Can you not imagine the effect it had on the peace of the household, the shouts, the endless footsteps on the stairs, the invasion of my study, the weeping? A whole afternoon's work ruined! What have you to say for yourselves?' His eye rested on Maria. 'As for you, young lady, I don't know whether you acted as Eve the temptress or whether they led you astray. I can only say that worse awaits you in your own home at the hands of the formidable Mrs Clomper.'

This means the end of Oxford and being sent back to school, thought Maria wretchedly. There was a sound of footsteps in the hall and Mrs Smith appeared behind the professor. 'How could you be so naughty, Thomas and Joshua? James so ill, and then you add to our anxiety by disappearing for so long. Come along in at once!' The door slammed shut behind them. Maria looked at it for a second and then up at the bedroom on the second floor. A muffled James waved at her cheerfully from behind the window. She walked as slowly as she could to the Lodgings, and went in by the door from the college quadrangle. The parlourmaid, who never had any fondness for Maria, came out of the kitchen with a trayload of glasses tinkling against each other. 'Well, Miss Maria, you're surely in for it, Mrs Clomper is that angry.'

'Where is she?' asked Maria in what she hoped was a carefree way.

'You'll find her in her room in a fair state.'

Maria walked briskly over the tiled hall while Amy was still in sight, and then dragged her feet over the thick red carpet on the stairs. She knocked at the door of the housekeeper's room and shut it very carefully behind her. 'Mrs Clomper, I've come back, and I'm sorry I was away for so long.'

The air in the room was stuffy and close, and the curtains had been half-drawn to keep out the sun. There was a strong smell of mothball. Mrs Clomper, who had a tea-tray beside her still, rose majestically from the armchair that was covered in a peculiarly dreary shade of brown plush. 'It is not me, Miss Maria, that your apologies are due to, but your uncle. That a gentleman of his learning and his position should have to be upset by the inconsiderate, wild behaviour of a little girl whom he is lodging in his house out of the kindness of his heart is a very shocking thing.' Having delivered herself of this formidable sentence, Mrs Clomper drew herself up and folded her arms. Maria's eye was wandering over the tea-tray, and she wondered however grown-ups could bear the sight of cold tea dregs in a slop basin. Then she was shocked at her irreverence at a moment of such crisis, and fixed her eyes abjectly on her shoes. 'I'm very sorry you were all so worried,' she murmured, 'and that we came back so late.'

'Worry, Miss Maria! It was not so much the worry as the disgrace. That you, the Warden's niece, a nicely brought-up young lady, should be seen careering through the streets of

Oxford in a farm cart in company with two little ruffians of boys and the kitchen-maid from the Lodgings! And Mrs Bastable, the porter's wife, coming round specially to tell me. I doubt whether the Lodgings will ever live down the disgrace. The poor Warden! How could you bring yourself to do it, Miss Maria? I want an answer.'

'But they weren't ruffians, they were the Smiths, and please don't blame poor Lizzie. We persuaded her to ask her uncle to take us. It was very kind of her.'

'Boys are always ruffians,' announced Mrs Clomper, 'and how a young lady could expose herself to their company in public passes my comprehension. As for Lizzie, I am perfectly aware, thank you, that the situation was not of her seeking. That girl hasn't the wits of a hedge sparrow. However, we shall have to try to teach her that her duties do not include taking the Warden's niece for rides.'

'Oh, poor Lizzie,' burst out Maria, 'you can't do that, please, you can't. She's so new and frightened.'

'Miss Maria, you exceed yourself.' Mrs Clomper swelled herself out. 'Are you trying to teach me my duties as the Warden's housekeeper, is that what you're trying to do?'

'Oh, no, please. I'm very sorry – but poor Lizzie.'

'You leave me to deal with Lizzie as I think fit, Miss Maria, and I shall leave the Warden to deal with you. Such turmoil we've been in, not knowing what had become of you, and the Warden's work interrupted through it all. Do you realize how essential it is, Miss Maria, that he should have peace of mind? All these years I have provided it for him and now you come, a naughty, rampageous little girl, and worry the life out of him.'

Maria was appalled at her own wickedness. 'Shall I go to Uncle Hadden now and apologize?'

'Apologize! There will be a lot more to do than that, that I can assure you! Let me see.' Mrs Clomper consulted the watch that was pinned to her chest. 'A quarter to seven. The Warden will be dining in Hall tonight. You had better go to his study at once before he goes up to change.'

Maria crept out of the room, and to her horror the door slipped out of her hand and banged shut. Now Mrs Clomper would think she was doing it on purpose. She went down the stairs one at a time and paused at the bottom. The portraits of past wardens hanging on the panelled walls of the hall looked at her severely. The handle of the study door rattled and the Warden appeared. He was brooding intently on something, his eyes fixed on the floor, and did not notice Maria. She stepped forward. 'Uncle Hadden, I've come to say I'm very sorry.' He gave a slight start and looked down at her. 'Ah, my dear Maria. You have come back, have you? Did you wish to see me? Let me see, I have five minutes in hand, have I not, before I need change for dinner.' He held back the study door for her, and then followed her in. Up till now Maria had never seen the study properly. It was a forbidding place. All round she was hemmed in by the dark calf bindings of row upon row of books. The Warden took up a position with his back to the window so that she could not see his face. 'Well?' he said questioningly. Maria backed against one of the shelves. Her hands clutched one another; they were damp with fright. 'I'm so very sorry that you were worried, and that I went in the cart with Lizzie,' she mumbled, not daring to look at him.

'The method of your going hardly matters, my dear Maria. The unfortunate thing is that it has caused Mrs Clomper some anxiety, and she is a worthy woman and has attended to my comfort for a good many years now, so I am reluctant to have her worried.'

Maria felt there was nothing more she could say; she would have far preferred Mrs Clomper's wrath to this mild manner. She fixed her eyes rigidly on one of the brass handles of the desk, and swallowed. There was a long pause.

'Whatever attraction was it that led you to spend the whole afternoon away from us?' went on the Warden.

Maria had never felt so hopelessly wicked in her life before; she remembered that if it had not been for her idiotic dare she and the Smiths would have spent a quiet afternoon in their respective gardens. 'We went to Long Slinfold,' she muttered, 'because of what I said to Thomas.'

'To Long Slinfold?' repeated the Warden in amazement. 'I confess I find it difficult to know what you could have said to Thomas Smith that would have taken you so far afield as Long Slinfold.' He paused but Maria was beyond giving an explanation. 'There is of course the Fitzackerley chapel in the church at Long Slinfold,' he added, more to himself than to her, 'but I hardly think you would have ventured so far merely for that. Besides, now I come to think of it, you were surely there yesterday. You told me, did you not, at breakfast yesterday that you were to be taken up to Jerusalem House by river with the young Smiths? Was it that you lost something there and wished to return to look for it?'

Maria shook her head miserably. This probing for a sensible reason for their escapade made the real explanation seem more impossible than ever to tell. 'I'm so sorry,' she repeated.

'Well, we must leave it at that, for our five minutes are up.' The Warden pulled a watch out of his pocket and pushed it back. 'Perhaps you will make your apologies to Mrs Clomper.' And he went over to the door and opened it for Maria to go through. She lingered in the hall, and heard her uncle walk heavily up the stairs, and his footsteps retreat along the passage; then she dragged her way up. There was a rustle at the top, and Mrs Clomper, awful in her black silk, appeared round the corner. 'Mrs Clomper, I'm really so sorry about what happened this afternoon,' said Maria, 'I'll never do it again, I promise. And I'm very sorry I banged the door when I went out. Really, I didn't mean to, it was an accident.'

'The banging of a door, Miss Maria, in itself is of no importance. But with you, I regret to say, it is a symptom of worse things. Take care to wash your face; and you had better change your dress at once.' And her back, terrifying in its rigidity, moved down the stairs.

When Maria went into her bedroom and saw her reflection in the tall glass fresh waves of misery broke over her. Her dress had long green stains down it, and there was a black smear by the side of her nose; what a thoroughly unpleasing object the Warden must have thought her! What Mrs Clomper thought hardly mattered, because whatever Maria did, she could never win her approval. Then a horrifying thought occurred to her; Mrs Clomper must have been on her way downstairs to scold poor Lizzie for her share in the afternoon's troubles. She had fully meant to tell Uncle Hadden about Lizzie, but the interview with him had been so miserable that she had never managed to say anything. Perhaps if she wrote him a note and left it where he was bound to find it? She tore out a page from her diary; there was no time to think carefully of the wording of the note, she just wrote: 'Please could you ask Mrs Clomper not to be angry with Lizzie for taking us to Long Slinfold in her uncle's cart. She did not really want to do it but we made her. She is very frightened of everybody.' She read it through hastily. Would Uncle Hadden know who Lizzie was? He was so remote from the affairs of this world. So she put a star against Lizzie, and underneath she wrote, 'Lizzie is a new maid here.'

She crept out of her bedroom with the note in her hand. The study door was open, Uncle Hadden was probably still dressing, and would go straight over to College Hall, and any place where the note would unfailingly catch his eye would also unfailingly catch Mrs Clomper's. She hovered at the top of the stairs, looking feverishly round, too anxious to think clearly. She could of course thrust it into his hand as he went downstairs on his way out, but explanations were bound to be asked for, and she felt she could not face any more of that tonight. She looked down the passage towards his dressing-room, and on a sudden impulse tiptoed up to the door and pushed the note through the crack underneath. Then she rushed back to her room.

When Amy brought up her supper half an hour later there was a note on the tray. Amy tapped it, 'From the Warden,' she said in a frivolous way. 'He's probably telling you that you've got to go back to school, but he's too kind to say it to you hisself.' Maria opened it with quivering hands. 'I think perhaps the young kitchen maid should be given an extra half day to make up for the one today that has been rather spoilt for her.' There was nothing more on the note, which was initialled H.H.H., and written in her uncle's beautiful handwriting. Maria let it fall on to the table. It was all right, nobody was going to punish Lizzie, but the note did make her feel more than ever ashamed.

She turned to her supper; it was obviously intended to be a punishment. There were some pieces of bread and butter that seemed to have been cut at breakfast time and exposed to every available ray of sun since then, and some sago pudding. There was also a glass of milk which had little pieces of sourish cream floating in it. Maria spread the sago on the bread and butter, which improved them both, she thought, but was defeated by the milk. She had a copy of *Quentin Durward* by her side, and hoped that if she read it with enough concentration she would find herself drinking the milk unknowingly. But in her present mood of misery it was impossible to read even a paragraph of the book, let alone forget how horrible the milk was. At last she went over to the window and looking cautiously out, poured it away. The milk trickled in a sluggish white stream over the Virginia creeper. How lucky it was that the purple wall-papered room that they had given to her as a sitting-room faced over the garden and not the quadrangle. She leant out, watching the cascade of milk, and then gave a violent start as she heard her name being called. On the wall Thomas was standing, signalling vigorously with both arms. With great agitation Maria tried to indicate to him that Mrs Clomper's room also overlooked the garden, and to beware.

'Are you all right?' he called. 'Was there a fearful rumpus?'

At that moment there was a rustle of silk below and she heard Mrs Clomper's voice. 'Get down from that wall this instant, young man. I won't have you there, disturbing the Warden in this audacious way.'

Maria fled into her bedroom, flung off her clothes, said her prayers with regrettable haste, and jumped into bed. She put her head under the bedclothes, and heard her heart hammering away. After a minute or so she came out of the stuffy darkness to gasp for air. The house was quite silent; Mrs Clomper seemed to have shut herself up in the house-keeper's room again. From the quadrangle outside she could hear undergraduates calling to each other, and then some-body came marching under her window singing 'Green Grow the Rashes O.' How happy and how heartless they all seemed, and she was so miserable. The song faded into the distance and Maria fell asleep.

The next day was Sunday; she awoke feeling burdened with gloom, and could not for the first moment remember why. Then it came back to her, everyone was very angry, and probably at this moment Uncle Hadden was considering whether he ought not to send her back to school. She was just about to go down to breakfast when, without bothering to knock, Amy banged her way in with a trayful of breakfast. 'Mrs Clomper's instructions, and she says as how you're to have breakfast up here by yourself, she says the Warden's had enough botheration from you to last him a lifetime, and let him have his breakfast in peace for once. Though why she can't punish you without punishing the person who's got to toil up here with your tray I can't say, I'm sure.' And she banged out again in a whirl of lilac print skirts.

Maria's mouth felt so dry that she could hardly manage to eat anything. How soon could they send her back to school? Surely not for a few days, by the time letters had been exchanged and her trunk packed. Perhaps she could redeem herself by really superb behaviour in the next day or two. Mrs Clomper said not a word to her as she escorted her to College Chapel later that morning. Maria looked furtively at Uncle Hadden. He sat serene in the Warden's Stall, by himself, a great purple cushion in front of him to bear the huge Prayer Book. His face showed no trace of anger, nor of anything else. In fact, he seemed completely unaware of his surroundings, and oblivious of the chorister who pattered down the aisle at intervals to turn over the pages of the Prayer Book for him.

Nothing was said on the way back from Chapel either, until they reached the door of the Lodgings. Then Mrs Clomper, looking severely in front of her, said, 'You will take luncheon today with the Warden as usual, Miss Maria.' Sunday was the one day of the week when Maria lunched with her uncle. Last Sunday had been the first occasion, and she had enjoyed it, for they expected little conversation of each other, and the Warden had poured her a glass of claret.

She did not much like the taste of this, but the colour was beautiful, and she loved the glasses engraved with vine leaves. But today it was going to be horrible, with the Warden presumably still angry from what had passed the day before. As she crept guiltily into the dining-room, her eyes fell on the engraving of Jerusalem House and she shuddered. Uncle Hadden was already in the room, gazing out of the window. He turned. 'Ah, Maria, I am glad to see you. You seemed not to be at breakfast, and I was afraid you were unwell.'

Muttering something about Mrs Clomper, Maria took her place, and the heavy Sunday lunch, with its roast lamb and onion sauce, followed by queen of puddings and wine jelly, went by without much further conversation. The Warden seemed abstracted, and Maria would never have dared talk to him, without being spoken to first. She wondered whether he was considering the question of school.

Sunday afternoon, for the Smiths as well as for Maria, was a period of repose before Evensong. The Smiths, who had attended morning service in the Cathedral because their father liked them to hear a good, intellectual sermon, in the evening went in procession to the college chapel, while Maria and Mrs Clomper went to Evensong in the Cathedral. Drowsy with the lunch, she wandered into the garden. For want of anything better to do she walked as far as the pear tree and called softly. The rope ladder was coiled round a branch of the pear tree, and the piece of string that would release it hung on the Smiths' side, so that she couldn't get up on to the wall unless there was a Smith about to deal with the ladder. The piece of string was Thomas's idea; you tied up the ladder in a bow with a very long piece of string, and then pulled at one of the ends to bring it down. She heard a scratching noise, and the ladder fell down. After a minute or so Joshua's head appeared.

'Hello,' he said, 'are you all right? Can anybody see me from your house?'

Maria shook her head, 'Not unless you stand on the wall. Mrs Clomper saw Mr Copplestone that day, and she saw Thomas yesterday.'

'Oh, well,' said Joshua, 'you could see Mr Copplestone from anywhere. He must find it a great disadvantage. Shall we climb up into the pear tree? Nobody could see us then. I'll get up first, and let the ladder down to you.'

The pear tree branches made comfortable seats, though they were rather too easy for climbing. Joshua and Maria settled themselves on branches that hung over the Smiths' garden. There was a leafy greenness round Maria, and a delicious rustling if she rocked the branch.

'What's Thomas doing?' Maria asked.

'Sticking in his stamps. He's in a terrible rage, and won't speak to me at all. Was Mrs Clomper very angry?'

'Yes, very – she still is. And I think Uncle Hadden was upset though he was so calm about it. He was upset because she was worried, and she was furious about us going in the cart, and because I had disturbed him. It's funny that they both worry so much about each other.' But Maria found that discussing it made the whole affair seem more ordinary, the sort of skirmish that the Smiths must regularly have in their household. 'The trouble is I can't tell whether Uncle Hadden's forgotten about it now or not. How did you get on? Your father seemed very angry.'

'That was chiefly because Mamma had been in such a state. I knew she would be, that was why I wanted to get home. We only had bread and butter for supper, and we can't have any cake for tea today, but I think Papa has calmed down now. He even made a joke this morning about the sermon. Thomas is in a terrible mood though.'

'But I saw him last night from my bedroom window, and

really he seemed in quite a good temper. He was waving to me.'

'He was all right then, until your Mrs Clomper came out into the garden and was so rude to him.'

All Maria's loyalty to the Lodgings and its inhabitants was roused by this attack by an outsider. 'She wasn't rude. She just told him to get down from the wall because he might disturb Uncle Hadden. She was quite right.'

'It's just as much our wall, and anyway the Warden wasn't there, he was having dinner in Hall, Papa said so. And you'd better not start defending Mrs Clomper to Thomas, you've no idea what he's like when he's in one of his moods.'

'Whose moods?' came a voice from below. Maria looked down. There was Thomas with his hands on his hips. 'Joshua, you're sitting in my place, get down.'

'Do you want to come up then?'

'It doesn't matter whether I do or not. But you can get down out of my place and find one of your own.'

'I'm not going to.' The only thing that ever stung Joshua into anger was unfairness. 'It's just as much my place as yours, you only sat there yesterday. If you wanted to come up I might give it to you, but I can see you don't.'

'Very well, then, you're asking for trouble.' Thomas clutched the trunk of the tree and began shaking it.

'This is lovely,' said Maria, 'the branches are swaying up and down, it's like a sort of lullaby.'

Thomas shook the tree more violently, a few leaves and baby pears fell down. Joshua broke off a bunch of these and began throwing them at his brother.

'Good heavens, Joshua, your aim is pretty poor, they're missing me by feet. Can't you do a little better than that?'

Maria seized a handful and began pelting. Her aim was fairly accurate. Thomas stopped shaking and surveyed them.

'There's worse punishment in store for you,' he announced. 'I warn you, I haven't begun yet.' He marched off.

'He's gone to get the clothes prop, I'm sure,' said Joshua. 'Quickly, Maria, let's get down and find some ammunition from your side of the wall. How about the compost heap? I saw a whole lot of cabbage stalks there.'

Thomas appeared with a seven-foot pole

They scrambled down to the wall. 'You stay on the wall,' said Maria, 'I'll hand up what I can find.' She scrabbled in the compost heap, and produced brussels sprout stalks, a few bulbs, and some conker cases from last autumn. 'Come on,' said Joshua. 'I can hear him coming.'

Rather excited at the thought of the siege she pulled herself up into the tree. Thomas appeared with a seven-foot pole, forked at the top. It was obviously not going to be safe to sit within range of it, so she and Joshua climbed up to the highest point in the tree, known as the Crow's Nest.

'Goodness, you can see Mrs Clomper's window from here,' said Maria with alarm.

'Is she there?' Joshua pretended not to notice Thomas's pole probing and rustling a few feet below them.

'No. She'll be having what she calls a "brief repose" now.'

'I.e., snoring,' said Joshua, 'and her window is tight shut too. I don't know how she can.'

There was a scrambling noise on the henhouse roof, and Thomas was standing on the wall. 'Aha, you can't escape now. I'll soon tickle you so that you wish you were on the ground.' Maria pulled a stalk out of Joshua's pocket and threw it down. It rattled through the leaves and plopped on to the henhouse. There was a startled scuffle of hens inside.

'Missed!' shouted Thomas. The clothes prop appeared among the leaves close to their heads. Joshua gingerly moved to a position farther from the wall. 'Come on, Maria, you'll be safe here as long as he stays on the wall.' They could only see Thomas's boots now through the leaves. There was a pause in the battle; Thomas was obviously planning his next attack. Then they heard footsteps approaching in the distance from the Lodgings side, and a familiar voice. 'How dare you rampage up there on a Sunday afternoon, disturbing everybody's peace. I've a had too much of this, young man, and I'm going to ask the Warden to speak to your father. Get down at once, and never let me see you up there again.' There was a jump on the henhouse, and Thomas was on the ground again. Joshua and Maria sat very still.

'Did she see the rope ladder?' asked Joshua urgently.

'Did she see us?' asked Maria.

'She couldn't have,' said Thomas, 'otherwise she would have confiscated the ladder and started on you too, for rampaging with us, and climbing trees on a Sunday, and heaven knows what else.' His voice was very bitter.

'Oh, I am sorry,' said Maria, slowly climbing down. 'She's always worrying about Uncle Hadden. I don't think he notices. He only gets upset if she's upset, and she always is.'

'It's lucky we didn't have James here,' said Thomas, 'capering about and adding one more boy to the scene. If you're a boy you can't do anything right in her eyes.'

'Girls can't do much right,' said Maria. 'At least, I can't.'

'Dear me, dear me, you look very chastened.' They all swung round, and saw the professor standing at the garden door. He wandered slowly down the steps and over the lawn towards them. He seemed in a very good humour. 'I shouldn't climb the pear tree if I were you, if that's what you were considering doing. Mrs Clomper might have something to say if you did.'

They looked guiltily at each other. 'She already has said a lot,' muttered Thomas to himself.

'Can it be that she *has* said something?' said the professor; he did not appear to be put out at the thought. 'I suppose she finds it rather trying in the summer, the season of open windows, and playing in the garden. But, my boys, remember poor Maria; she is the one who suffers, I feel sure, when you three annoy Mrs Clomper in any way. And I am quite certain that she had enough of Mrs Clomper yesterday to last her a lifetime. Isn't that so, Maria?'

Maria hung her head and wished that he would stop. 'Never mind,' went on the professor briskly. 'If you find being good too difficult, you'll have to concentrate on being clever. Mr Copplestone tells me that you are making excellent progress; I passed on the news to your uncle last night, and he was delighted, positively delighted. And while I am on the subject of delight, I have news for you; James has not got scarlet fever, the doctor has just told us so. So he will be able to join you for lessons tomorrow as usual, Maria.'

'I wish James wasn't always right,' grumbled Thomas after his father had gone back into the house. 'It's so bad for him, and he'll boast for weeks now about everybody saying he had scarlet fever when he knew he hadn't.'

'It would have been nice to have had lessons without him just for one day,' said Joshua. 'Don't you think so, Maria?'

But Maria did not really care; she was far too pleased at hearing of her uncle's approval to bother about James.

CHAPTER SEVEN

Original Research

When James appeared at Monday's lessons he was apparently none the worse for his illness, except that his temper was rather bad. It was a hot and cloudless day and, as he had already pointed out to his parents, his brothers, and Nurse, because he had spent the week-end in bed (two fine days too), he felt he was entitled to have the first two days of the week free from lessons.

'I'm glad you didn't get scarlet fever,' said Maria politely.

'I knew I wouldn't. I told them I wouldn't. Nothing ever happens to me when I don't want it to.'

'Anybody can prevent a thing happening once they are aware of the danger,' said Mr Copplestone airily. 'One only needs a little concentration. I concentrate for eight and a half minutes before breakfast, myself. The trouble comes when things take you by surprise.'

'How do you mean?' James's temper was rising. He resented Mr Copplestone taking the wind from his sails.

'They thought you were going to get scarlet fever. You said you would not, and concentrated on not getting it, and the rest was easy. But supposing you had no idea there was any danger, that the germ stole up and took you unawares, and there you were laid low, all spotty, too late to will it away. What then?'

'That hasn't happened to me.'

'And let us hope it will never happen to you, dear boy ... And on this occasion, though Miss Maria and I may not feel so thankful at your excellent recovery as perhaps we ought, we can feel it is your nurse's gain.'

A faint smile appeared on Maria's face, but she quickly suppressed it, because she did not want to make James's temper any worse. James sat up very stiffly, examining both their faces, rather unsure what the joke was about.

'And now, *discipulae meae*,' said Mr Copplestone, 'we will to our Public School Latin Primer. James, if you can concentrate on that for an hour without a single word on any other subject, I'll treat you to two pennyworth of sherbert fizzers, only you must give one quarter to Maria, because she is always good.'

But neither with the Public School Latin Primer nor with the Greek Primer could Maria do any good this morning. It seemed as though all that she had previously learnt had been swept from her brain. She produced the verb endings of the French past definite tense when she was asked for the future tense of *moneo*, until, when she was confronted with the simple Greek sentence of ἔχουσι ἵππους τινας, not only was she completely unable to translate it, she could not even pronounce it, the letters to her eye suddenly became as meaningless as an inscription in Arabic.

'I won't have to give her any sherbert fizzers now, will I?' said James triumphantly.

'You will,' said Mr Copplestone, 'because she has been good if not sparkling with intelligence.'

'I've never known anybody be so stupid,' said James. He was in a horrible mood this morning.

'Far better to be stupid and good than clever and evilly disposed,' said Mr Copplestone. 'Or so one has to tell people in sermons. But this is not stupidity, it is the beginning of complete loss of memory, I am afraid. Do you remember what your name is?' he asked Maria. She just gazed at him dumbly, far too miserable to say anything.

'She doesn't know,' said James. 'Maria, do you know where you live? Do people ever get their memory back when it's lost, or do they have to go to lunatic asylums?'

Luckily for Maria, Thomas and Joshua came upstairs then, and as it was too hot for Mr Copplestone to think of anything else, he set James on to drawing pictures of Crusaders and battles, while the other three took in turns to read paragraphs aloud from their history text book.

Between the end of lessons and lunch the four children went to lie under the apple trees at the bottom of the garden. It was difficult to persuade James not to go round to Mrs Knight's to buy his first halfpennyworth of sherbert fizzers. (He was saving the other three-halfpence for the time being.)

'They would be no good to you, Jas,' said Joshua, 'you aren't allowed to eat them until after lunch, anyway.'

'I could lick them. Mamma has never said anything about licking sweets before meals. I'd let you lick too, Jos, if you would come with me to buy them now. Besides, I want to eat one immediately after lunch, and I couldn't unless I bought them now.'

'It's no good, I'm not coming now. It really is most unfair that you always get rewarded for being thoroughly naughty,' said Joshua lazily.

'I was very good today,' said James huffily. 'That was why I was rewarded.' He looked balefully at Maria. 'And I've got to give a quarter to *her*, and you can't think how stupid she was. She couldn't do a single thing in Greek – not even read the letters, and in Latin . . .'

'That's enough, James,' ordered Thomas, 'or I'll tell Maria how often you used to cry two years ago.'

'I was trying too hard, that was the trouble,' said Maria bitterly. She was lying with her face propped in her hands, chewing a grass stem. 'I tried so hard that I thought my head would burst, but I couldn't remember anything about anything. It was just like being at school.'

'I think James ought to give a quarter of his fizzers to each of us,' said Thomas. 'We were both thoroughly well-behaved, and nobody dreams of rewarding us – and it's hard pounding doing lessons with Papa, too.'

'I wish he wouldn't walk round and round the table so

'I'll lick all the rest so that you can't eat them'

fast when I try to think what something means,' said Joshua. 'It makes me very nervous.'

James was very put out at the thought of a possible raid on his fizzers. 'I'm not going to give you a quarter each. I'll give you one each, perhaps, but I won't promise, and I'll lick all the rest so that you can't eat them. It's probably a reward from heaven anyway because you were so naughty on Saturday, and I was so ill and good.'

'Mr Copplestone's not my idea of heaven,' said Joshua. But Thomas sat up with a jerk. 'Good! You were just about as badly behaved as you possibly could be, inside the limits of a bedroom. You nearly drove Nurse into a lunatic asylum. Her hair was much whiter this morning, I noticed. In fact I'm surprised it didn't fall out overnight into her pillow.' Joshua and Maria giggled. James ignored them. 'Anyway, you were all dreadful on Saturday. Poor Mamma,' he added smugly. 'I'm sure *her* hair's greyer because of you. I expect Papa was very angry with you.'

'Not particularly,' said Thomas casually.

'Papa was angry,' contradicted James. 'I could hear what he said to you on the doorstep. He called you wretched miscreants. What is a miscreant?'

'What you are.'

'Wretched miscreant,' said Joshua, poking James in the ribs.

James took no notice, but turned towards Maria. 'Maria, your hair is full of grass,' he announced, taking the opportunity to add a few more pieces as she lay there.

'I think it looks rather pretty,' said Joshua, turning his head lazily to look at her, 'very rustic. Doesn't the grass look tall when you lie in it. There must be millions of spiders and things in it that we can't see, busily living their little lives.'

'I wonder if they realize that we're around,' said Maria idly.

'I shouldn't think their eye could take in anything so vast,' Thomas asserted. 'A blade of grass is probably as high as they can see, and after that a bit of our leg looks like a thundercloud on the horizon.'

'Do you think that there are giants round us, too big for us to see, but watching us and poking us with bits of grass?'

'Highly improbable,' said Thomas.

'I don't see why not,' James objected. 'The spiders can't see us, we can't see the giants. How do you know there aren't any?'

'I'm not going to argue with you, James, however much you want it. Don't be so tiresome.'

'That's because you know you are always beaten. You're just like Miss Gracie. I'm going to be a really great man when I grow up, a genius.'

'How are you going to be a great man, Jas?' Joshua asked, while Thomas was still groaning with disgust at this latest example of James's impossible arrogance.

'I don't know. It will just show itself when I'm grown up. But I shall be.'

Thomas stopped groaning. 'Poor old Jas. You are going to have a bitter time when you get to Rugby. You'll be Smith minimus then – the least Smith, and you'll get so trodden on, and it won't be any good coming to Jos or me for help. You just don't know what is in store for you.'

'I'll just knock everyone down.'

'It's going to be horrible being Smith minor while he's there,' said Joshua while Thomas was laughing contemptuously at James's idea of how to get on at school, 'he'll always be doing perfectly dreadful things.'

'Do you *want* to go to school?' asked Maria.

'Yes,' said Thomas without hesitation. 'Of course.'

'Everybody has to go to school,' said Joshua.

'If they sent me now,' said Maria, 'it would be just as a punishment.'

'As a punishment?' Joshua queried. 'What for?'

'Oh, for getting in Uncle Hadden's way, and stopping him working properly. And for not being any good at the sort of lessons I do with Mr Copplestone. That was why I particularly wanted to do well this morning after everyone had been so cross with me on Saturday, and said I interfered with Uncle Hadden's work. And your father said that if I couldn't be good I ought to try to be clever. And look what happened,' Maria finished dolefully. 'I forgot everything I had ever learnt. If Mr Copplestone tells Uncle Hadden, Uncle Hadden will naturally think it's a waste of time teaching me Latin and Greek and send me back to school.'

'Oh, don't worry,' said Thomas. 'I'm sure the Streak won't tell your uncle anything. He doesn't take our lessons seriously enough. Mr Ledgard, our real tutor, takes them very seriously, though.'

'But he told your father, and your father told Uncle Hadden, that I was making good progress. What is he going to tell him after this morning?' Pursued Maria gloomily.

'Can't you do something superb, just to show?' suggested Joshua.

'Such as what? It's no good just trying hard at lessons, it simply doesn't work.'

'Original research,' said James, who was lying on his back waving his legs in the air.

His brothers set on him. 'What do you know about original research? You don't even know what it means.'

'Of course I know. It's finding out about things that nobody else knows about.'

'What sort of things?'

'If you discovered who that "Unknown Boy" was. The one in the drawing that we saw in the house the Streak took us to.'

'And what happens when you do know?' Maria asked.

'You write a learned paper about it, like Papa does, and read it aloud somewhere. I could do it easily if I wanted to.'

Thomas flung himself at James and was just about to shake him with great violence, when the sound of the gong reached them. 'At last,' Thomas said, scrambling to his feet. 'The hunger of me! I wonder what's for lunch.'

'Cold lamb, beetroot, potatoes, treacle tart,' said James, 'I asked Cook. She gave me a slice of bread and dripping too. It was because I was ill.'

'I wish it wasn't going to be beetroot,' said Joshua plaintively.

They always took luncheon in the dark brown dining-room in the company of Mr Copplestone and Mrs Smith, who presided when the professor was lunching, as he usually did, in college. But on this occasion he was present. 'The Warden is bringing a particularly intolerable politician in to luncheon today, and I really think that cold mutton and the presence of my family will for once be preferable to the common room.' He beamed round at them benevolently. 'The most boring man I have ever met. Don't any of you boys dare to be politicians when you grow up. James, will you say grace.'

'Papa,' said James when they had all sat down, 'could I write a learned paper, do you think?'

'Provided you have the learning, my dear boy. And a thirst for learning is really what is needed. (The red-currant jelly, if you please, Joshua.) I don't know if you have that. What do you say about it, Copplestone?'

Mr Copplestone was absorbed in cutting a round of beetroot into a five-pointed star, and gave a start. 'About the thirst for learning, Professor? There is a thirst for *knowledge* – and rather useless knowledge – in one or two of your sons, to a positively embarrassing degree.' (Here he looked at James.) 'In fact, I find it exceedingly difficult to stem the ceaseless flow of questions.'

James ignored all this. 'Could Maria write learned papers? She wants to.'

Maria bent her crimson face over her plate of cold mutton. 'I didn't say I wanted to, James.'

'It's certainly what the Warden wants her to do,' said

Professor Smith looking at her amiably. 'In fact, he intends her to be my successor in the Chair of Ancient History. There's nothing like an early start to your endeavours, Maria.'

'She wants to do research about that house Mr Copplestone took us to,' said James relentlessly. Maria had never realized until this moment how embarrassed it was possible to be.

'Research at Jerusalem House may be rather difficult.' Mr Copplestone had completed his beetroot star, and was now taking off the points one by one and nibbling them like a canary. 'Shall we say that the worthy Miss Hickmott, custodian of the house, regards us as dangerous revolutionaries whose great object is to set fire to the house and pillage its treasures. Or she behaves as though she thought this.'

'I know,' said James, 'let's all go there disguised. I could wear a wig.'

'You'll do nothing of the sort, James,' said his mother. 'There is no need for any of you to go to Jerusalem House again; besides, that is probably how you caught your chill. No, you can't have any of that sauce; it's for your Papa, only gentlemen eat that.'

'When will I be a gentleman? When I go to school or when I am twenty-one?'

'Never,' said Thomas with great decision. 'Mamma, shall I ring the bell for Laura?'

'If everyone has quite finished,' said Mrs Smith, sweeping a disapproving look at Mr Copplestone, on whose plate a piece of beetroot still remained. 'No, Joshua has not. Come along, Joshua, eat up your beetroot, I only gave you a very little, and it's so good for you.'

'Why is beetroot good for you, Papa?' asked James.

'Ask your Mamma, James my boy, she is much better

versed in such matters. For my part I wonder why Nature created the beetroot, it seems a highly unnecessary vegetable. Now, to return to research, Maria, there are several conditions essential before you can undertake it. Firstly, peace and quiet, and there I imagine you are luckier than I am. Secondly, a library – and you have a splendid one under your roof, and thirdly a subject you are passionately interested in. Now, is there anything you are passionately interested in?' Maria shook her head. 'That's bad, bad,' said the professor. 'Everybody should have a passionate interest, even if it's only climbing trees; something you pursue single-mindedly.'

'Like James pursues sherbert fizzers,' put in Thomas.

'I doubt whether after all this poor Maria wants to pursue anything single-mindedly,' said Mr Copplestone, as the parlourmaid took away his plate, still decorated with rejected pieces of beetroot, 'except the destruction of James.'

CHAPTER EIGHT

A Bet on Maria

THE second week with Mr Copplestone produced weather as fine and hot as he had prophesied it was going to be. They sat over lessons with the schoolroom windows flung up, and the sound of the multitudinous bells of Oxford drifting in to them, bells calling to chapel, to lunch, calling out the time. James slumped in his chair and said he was too hot to work, and Mr Copplestone gave up bull-fighting on most days, and instead drew little sketches to show them what matadors wore, and the sort of people you would find in a bull-fighter's audience. When Thomas and Joshua came up from lessons with their father, they would usually find Maria leaning back in her chair gazing out of the window, and James feverishly writing out things to earn some reward. They found it pleasant to relax after strenuous sessions with their father, and hours that should have been devoted to history or maths were more often spent listening to Mr Copplestone's accounts of what he did at school, which seemed to have been an eccentric establishment of about fifteen boys in a country vicarage. At least Joshua listened, while Thomas brooded over Rugby, and whether he was going to like it, and James examined the scratches and scars he had so far acquired this summer, and reckoned they were disappointingly few by last summer's standards. Maria bit her pencil, and listened to Mr Copplestone with half her attention but let her thoughts wander away to what James had said about research. If she could really find out who that boy in the picture was, and give a lecture on it which her uncle would attend without knowing that his niece was the lecturer, then surely he would consider her as promising! Or even if she could write something about it and leave it on his desk for him to discover. But first, how did you find out what you wanted to know, and secondly, having found it out, what did you write? Obviously a paper had to be rather longer than 'The picture is of ... by ...' Nervously, she tackled Joshua about this point a couple of days after James had first raised the matter of original research. She did not much trust him as an authority, but there was nobody else that she dared ask.

'You say who it is, and why you think it is, and put in all kinds of insulting things about the other people who don't agree with you,' Joshua told her.

'I suppose I could insult Miss Hickmott then. I must say, I would like to. But the trouble is I don't know how to start proving anything. I only know that Thomas said the boy reminded him of the other portraits in the room.'

'I suppose you could go and look at it again, it might give you an idea,' said Joshua without much enthusiasm, 'or ask Mr Copplestone.'

But Maria did not in the least want to ask anybody, certainly not Mr Copplestone. If she was going to do research, it would be without help. That afternoon, as they were arguing hotly whether Mary Queen of Scots was good or bad, Maria scribbled idly on her blotting paper what she did know about the picture, which only amounted to the fact that it was a drawing which hung in Jerusalem House. This looked very thin, so she added the inscription and the date which she had discovered carved in the stone, and then the words 'Deborah Fitzackerley, died 1652 aged 10'. She drew heavy pencil rings round each of these three statements and frowned down at them. The trouble was that they had nothing to do with each other; the drawing of the unknown boy might belong to any century. Then it suddenly came over her that the Deborah of the tablet in the church and the Deborah with the cockatoo on her arm, standing with her brother in Jerusalem House, were surely both referred to as the daughter of the ninth Lord Fitzackerley, therefore they must be the same person. And this meant that the little Stephen Fitzackerley standing beside his sister could have been the hand that carved an inscription in the parapet in 1654, as she had suggested to Thomas. Perhaps, after all, it was not such a wild theory; in fact it would be worth concentrating on finding out more about it, and giving up the unknown boy. She triumphantly raised her head to find that everybody had stopped arguing and were all looking at her with curiosity.

'Now Maria has no views on the ill-starred Queen of the Scots,' said Mr Copplestone. 'It seems to be a subject that interests us men only.'

'I think it's rather boring,' said James.

'That's because you're only a little boy,' Thomas told him. 'Little boys only like eating sweets.'

'I myself think that enough has been said on the subject,' announced Mr Copplestone. 'How about a lesson on navigation tomorrow? We haven't had a geography lesson yet, now I come to think of it.'

'Geography!' Maria murmured under her breath, remembering the last disastrous geography lesson at Semphill House.

'I mean in the shape of a little exercise on the river,' Mr Copplestone proceeded. 'In this heat it would be very suitable, and besides, I have neglected the physical culture side of your education.'

'Do you think we could spend the whole afternoon on the river, sir?' Joshua asked. 'We could do lessons there just as well as here – it would be so much cooler. We could all take our history books and things.'

'We shall see,' said Mr Copplestone, 'which being interpreted means, on the whole I am inclined to say, yes.'

This was Thursday, and as Maria walked back to the Lodgings to have tea with Uncle Hadden, the blotting paper with her notes folded up inside her Greek exercise book, it came over her that the next day, Friday, was the day the public was admitted to Jerusalem. Suppose Mr Copplestone could be persuaded to row up the river in that direction (after all, there only were two directions you could row on a river), and she could slip away from the boat at Jerusalem House, then she could make quite certain from the tablet in the church and from the picture of the two children that they did both refer to 'the ninth Lord Fitzackerley'.

She spent Friday morning in a fever of anxiety about the afternoon's arrangements. At one moment it seemed the easiest thing in the world to suggest subtly that their navigation lesson took them in the direction of Jerusalem House, and at the next extremely unlikely that Mr Copplestone would choose to row upstream. It was exceedingly hot, so hot that all one wanted to do was to creep from shadow to shadow. They could feel the heat of the pavement through the soles of their boots as they walked to Timms' boathouse after lunch carrying history books and an atlas under their arms. Maria dragged behind with Joshua. 'Look, Jos,' she urged, 'do you think we could go up the river in the same direction as we did last Friday? Could you suggest it, do you think?'

But Joshua was feeling the heat. 'Why don't you suggest it?'

'They're your brothers, they'd take it better from you.'

'We always do what Thomas wants. Why not ask him?'

'Oh, Jos, please! Well, if I suggest it, will you back me up?'

'But what does it matter anyway?'

'You see, I do so very much want to see Jerusalem House again.'

'Jerusalem House!' said Joshua with horror. 'But it's miles away, and a lot of the way there's no shade at all. I hope we don't go as far as that.'

With a sigh Maria gave it up. Mr Copplestone had James bounding beside him, questioning him about how many people were killed at bull-fights, and Thomas was striding along by himself in a rather irritable and distant mood; she would just have to wait until they were in the boat, and chance it that they rowed off in the right direction.

At the boathouse, James had decided ideas about what boat they should take, very fantastic ideas, and his brothers opposed him. The wrangle might have gone on for some time, if Mr Copplestone had not created a diversion.

'A Cambridge man!' He sounded so indignant that everybody swung round in his direction. He was standing like one transfixed, his eyes glassily on the river. The only thing to be seen was a young man in beautiful white flannel trousers and a blazer, with a purple and yellow ribbon round his boater, clumsily trying to propel his punt from the stern instead of the conventional Oxford position in front. 'Intruding on our river! Making himself conspicuous like that – who does he think he is, the frightful fellow!'

The man in the purple and yellow boater, who could hear every word, and feel the ten eyes on him, was becoming more and more confused, and the ladies with him, who looked as though they might be his aunts, were murmuring indignantly. Joshua tried to pacify Mr Copplestone. 'He couldn't go down to the other end now, he would trample on the ladies. Shall we have this boat?'

They clambered in as it bobbed by the landing stage, and Mr Copplestone took the oars, casting a last indignant look at the Cambridge man, who was now in difficulties, his punt sideways across the river, one end stuck in the bank. There was a moment or two's pause while they settled themselves; Maria tried feverishly to work out whether Mr Copplestone was sitting in the right direction for going upstream, but she could not remember which way rowers faced. But the first obstacle was removed. Mr Copplestone started off in the right direction, though Maria held her breath in case one of the boys should start objecting. The first reaches of the river were crowded with punts. Mr Copplestone surveyed them with displeasure, they got in his way, and none of the punters these days, he remarked, seemed to know their job, they looked so inelegant. People turned round to gaze at their boat as he pulled upstream. His enormous height, capped by a small boater bearing the M.C.C. colours – red and liverish yellow – made him very conspicuous. Men lounging in punts moored by the banks lifted their eyes from their books to look at him curiously, young ladies looked at him from under their parasols, and asked their escorts if they knew who he was.

'Do many people know you here, sir?' asked Joshua. 'They look as if they did.'

'I have a fair number of acquaintances,' said Mr Copplestone rather crossly, 'but none of them is, I am thankful to say, on the river this afternoon.'

His temper seemed to be suffering from the heat too, thought Maria. The vivid green of the country had dulled since last week, and looked dusty and worn. James leaned dangerously over the side, pulling at rushes and plants by the fringe of the river. Joshua looked at him anxiously, but decided it was wiser to say nothing. They had left the punts behind them. Surely any minute now we shall be seeing Jerusalem House, Maria thought.

'It's like the inside of a potter's kiln,' said Mr Copplestone. He removed his boater and wiped his face with its brim. 'James, if you fall out, none of us will mind in the least, but you'll have to make up your mind to stay there among the rushes until we come back this way.'

Thomas pulled at James's jacket to try to bring more of him into the boat, and James came back with a bad grace. 'When are we going home to tea?' he demanded. 'I'm so hot, I'll either have to take off all my clothes or die.' He looked at them closely: 'I think you'd rather I died.'

Mr Copplestone rested on his oars. 'Our friend James has a point there, if not two points; tea and the heat. When shall we start our lesson?'

There was a dismal silence. They had forgotten about the nagivation lesson, and the history books thrown on the bottom of the boat. 'Could we just stay here under this willow tree,' suggested Thomas, 'and dip our feet in the water.'

'And then tea,' added James.

Maria looked anxiously at Joshua and tried to will him to speak up for her. As he took no notice she nudged him with her foot.

'Oh, Maria wants us to go on,' Joshua announced, 'she wants to go as far as Jerusalem House, or something.'

'All the Smiths are exactly like their father,' Maria thought angrily, 'they all say the most embarrassing things possible.'

'To Jerusalem House!' Thomas and James shouted. 'Maria, we can't! It's miles farther on. Whatever do you want to do there?'

Mr Copplestone looked at Maria. 'The noes have it, and even if I didn't let them have it, to row three angry young males up as far as that, would be torture, utter torture. It's quite bad enough rowing them back,' he said crossly. 'And it's no good asking me if you can dip your feet in the river; if you did you would only all catch scarlet fever and whooping cough with complications, and your mamma would say that it was my fault.'

And so they turned round and rowed back. Maria looked wistfully back over her shoulder, towards the fields they were leaving, and was certain that only five minutes' more rowing would have brought them in sight of the house. Or if they would wait, she could run there. But she did not dare say anything, and every oar stroke was taking them nearer Oxford.

'I suppose something should be done about a lesson of some sort,' said Mr Copplestone, after about a quarter of an hour's silence. 'I agree with you all that it's a thoroughly distasteful subject, but there is my duty to your father to consider. Well, look here.' He stopped rowing and pointed vaguely into the sky. 'There is the sun, navigators steer by the sun and the stars. I haven't the faintest notion how, but you can puzzle it out for your homework tonight.' There was a great smack of water. 'Oh, James! As sure as tadpoles become frogs, I knew you would do that before the afternoon was out.'

James, who had taken advantage of the halt to try to grab a baby moorhen, was now floundering in the water. 'He'll drown, he'll drown!' shrieked Joshua trying to stand up and rocking the boat wildly. 'Sit down, you fool,' said Thomas, grabbing at him, 'or you'll have all of us in. Maria, try to grab at James while I hold down Joshua.'

But James was threshing with his arms wildly just out of Maria's reach. She leaned dangerously over the gunwales as Mr Copplestone tried to bring the boat near him. He was near the rushes at the edge of the river now, but as his eyes were tight shut in his panic there was no chance that he

'He'll drown, he'll drown!' shrieked Joshua

would have the sense to try to scramble out that way. 'Oh, thank goodness, there are two men coming up on the bank,' panted Maria, looking up for a moment. The men took in the situation at a glance, one of them lay on the bank while the other held him firm, and James was hauled on to dry earth.

'Oh, thank you,' said Maria fervently.

'Shake him hard,' said Mr Copplestone grimly to the two men, 'until I can bring the boat into position to take on this monstrous child. Gentlemen, we are very much obliged to you.'

James was not at all ashamed of himself when he climbed back into the boat. His hair was plastered in red streaks over his face, his clothes dripped into the bottom of the boat, while he talked excitedly of how cool it had been in the water, and how it had been the best part of the whole afternoon.

'Don't be so silly, James,' said Joshua with exasperation, 'you were absolutely terrified, shrieking and waving your arms about.'

'That was because I was enjoying it so much. And of course I had to pretend I was frightened to make it more exciting.'

'Why on earth didn't we leave him in the river?' said Thomas. 'And have you thought of what you're going to say to Mamma when she sees you all wet? She'll never let you go near a river again.'

'I'll dry by the time I get home.'

'Oh, no, you won't,' said Joshua. 'Thomas, we'll have to try and keep it from Mamma. Perhaps we could dry his things in the attic without anybody finding out.'

On the way from Bardwell Road to Canterbury Lane James, with squelching noises coming from his sodden boots, marched between his two brothers, with Mr Copplestone in front and Maria behind him, to try to hide him. She left them outside their house, debating how best to get James upstairs unnoticed, and went into the Lodgings. She dragged up the stairs feeling cross and miserable. She had never been so hot in her life, all the starch had gone out of her dress and it clung to her damply, and strands of hair flopped in her eyes and tickled her face. The Warden was not going to be able to have tea with her today, so after gulping down the milk that had been left for her in her sitting-room, and eating the scones and damson jam and the Madeira cake, she began on her homework. Her views about how ships used the sun and the stars to steer by were vaguer even than Mr Copplestone's. She remembered with horror how she had never been able to grasp from the geography lessons at Semphill House what the sun did and why day was day and night was night. Then, with sudden inspiration she wrote: 'From earliest times men have found their way by the stars. The Three Magi . . .' She wrote the story in her largest writing to fill up a page, and under it put 'No more time', and turned thankfully to her Greek.

Amy brought in her supper with the usual banging of doors and slamming down of trays. 'Cook couldn't be bothered to do much for you today, the Warden's got a lot of gentlemen coming to dinner, a very big do, and seven courses, and she's nearly beside herself.' They had sent up a plate of rather dry cold mutton and a tomato. But on the other hand, there were quite a lot of broken meringue shells. She had pushed away the tray and was staring vacantly out of the window and wondering whether she had enough energy to write up her diary when Mrs Clomper bustled into the room. 'What a day to look like a bedraggled little waif when the Warden is entertaining and has specially asked for you,' she said, eyeing her with deep disapproval. 'You had better come along to your bedroom and let me do something about your hair.' Mrs Clomper had a heavy hand, and her brush strokes made Maria wince. Then she wrenched with a comb, and finally Maria was told to put on her blue hair ribbon and her embroidered white muslin. Amy would come to tell her when dessert had been taken in. The Warden was entertaining gentlemen who had known her father, and he thought (though Mrs Clomper clearly could have told him better) that they might be interested to see her.

When Maria dressed herself in her white muslin she went to sit in the window seat in her sitting-room and brooded over the ordeal that lay ahead of her. The idea of walking into the dining-room was terrifying. Suppose that nobody noticed her and she had to stand like an image, waiting to be seen! Worse still, if the guests saw her but the Warden did not, and they all stared at her curiously, wondering whoever she could be.

Then Amy came in with a hurried knock. 'Your uncle says you're to come down now. My word, just look at your hands, all over ink. Well, he's waiting for you so don't you spend too long cleaning yourself.' And off she bounced. Maria could hear her footsteps tit-tupping rapidly downstairs as she rubbed uselessly at her ink-stained fingers with a sponge in her bedroom. It did not really matter, she thought, she could easily keep her hands behind her back the whole time.

She paused for a minute outside the dining-room door. There was a deep babble of men's voices and laughter. She fingered the handle. In an hour, she thought, it will all be over, but in one moment I shall be inside.

'Go on, for lawk's sake, Miss Maria,' hissed Amy from the kitchen passage. 'Whatever do you think you're waiting for?'

So in she went. She stood there on the cushiony red Axminster. There was a sea of faces on either side of the long table, and the sound of the cracking of nuts and much talk. The Warden had his back to her. She went and stood timidly by his chair. 'Ah, there you are, my dear Maria. These two gentlemen have asked particularly to see you, Mr Benson and Mr Hardwicke. They knew your father at New College.' The Warden indicated two faces on his right. Before Maria had recovered from the shock of being sent for by two strangers, she had a second shock. These two faces were the men who had rescued James from the river this afternoon. They looked at her closely, and then the face that the Warden had introduced as Mr Hardwicke, turned to the other and said, 'The half-sovereign's mine.'

'Well, well,' said the other man, Mr Benson. 'Who would have credited it?' And they stared at Maria again, until she dropped her eyes with embarrassment. 'We had a bet on you,' said Mr Hardwicke after a long pause. 'When we met you over the rescuing of your young friend, I thought I recognized your face and swore that you must be the daughter of John Henniker-Hadden, you looked so remarkably like him; he was up at New College at the same time as we were.'

'And I swore you couldn't be,' said Mr Benson, who had ginger, drooping whiskers. 'Couldn't imagine what you were doing in a boat with three little boys and that madman Copplestone. I still can't imagine. So we asked the Warden to produce you to settle the question. But why are you in the clutches of Copplestone?'

'Mr Copplestone is our tutor while our other one is away,' said Maria nervously.

'And who is "we"?'

'Thomas, Joshua, and James Smith and me.'

There was another long pause, and then the Warden, looking in their direction and seeing that the conversation seemed to be dragging, tried to help. 'Maria went to Jerusalem House last week,' he said to Mr Benson, and then to Maria: 'Mr Benson is studying the family papers of the Fitzackerleys. You will find he knows a great deal about the house.'

'Does Miss Hickmott allow you inside her fortress then?' asked Mr Benson.

Maria lifted her eyes for a moment to look at him. 'She does on Fridays.' Then she remembered what had happened the week before. 'But I don't think we could ever go again, she thinks we behave very badly.'

'The effect of Copplestone, no doubt,' said Mr Hardwicke to Mr Benson.

'Do you know a lot about the Fitzackerley family?' asked Maria timidly, looking at them both, and clutching her inky hands firmly behind her back in case she forgot about them and brought them to the front where they could be seen.

'He does,' said Mr Hardwicke, indicating Mr Benson. 'He's writing a history of some of them. I'm just a dull dog of a mathematician.'

Here was a heaven-sent opportunity. 'Do you know anything about a Stephen Fitzackerley?' Maria asked Mr Benson eagerly, having smiled politely at Mr Hardwicke. 'I think he may have lived in 1654.'

'Ah, I don't deal with the seventeenth-century Fitzackerleys. I'm really only concerned with the early part of the family's history, up to Elizabeth's reign.' He gazed vacantly across the table. 'Of course I do come across some of the later correspondence as I plough through the papers. Stephen Fitzackerley? No one of that name succeeded to the title – but no doubt you know that. What you need is the family tree. Or there is an account of the seventeenth-century Fitzackerleys written about fifty years ago; you would find it in Bodley. They were an interesting lot. Richard, the ninth lord, was one of the Cavalier poets, and collected a group of learned men around him. He also laid out a lot of the garden.'

'Did this ninth lord have a daughter called Deborah?' broke in Maria, 'she died when she was ten.'

Mr Benson shook his head. 'Oh, I can't tell you that. But you would find it all out from this book, and track down your Stephen too. I imagine he's a son who died in infancy.'

'I think he must have been a son of the ninth lord,' said Maria.

'Oh?' said Mr Benson, without much interest.

'Do you like walnuts?' said Mr Hardwicke, offering her one. 'Must say I have a passion for them myself, and for crystallized fruit. Have one of these apricots.' Maria took them awkwardly in her left hand, which she remembered as being the least inky. Soon after this they seemed to lose interest in her. Maria presented herself at her uncle's elbow again, and said, 'Shall I go now, Uncle Hadden?'

'I should think so, my dear,' said the Warden. 'Thank you for coming down to see us.' And Maria shut the noise of voices behind the door, and went up to bed.

CHAPTER NINE

Bodley and the Bull

WHERE and what was Bodley, Maria wondered when she woke up on Saturday morning. Of course, Mr Benson might have been referring to her uncle's library, and she supposed she ought to look there first. So after breakfast she waited until the Warden had shut himself into the study and she felt she would be undisturbed in the library. She started by the door, crouching down to examine the bottom shelf, and dutifully looked at every title in the row. But they all seemed to be books in Latin. She reached the end of the shelf and wearily stood up with cramped legs; there were thousands more books and she could never look at every one. Besides, there did not seem to be anything in the library, she thought, as she wandered round it, on a subject like the one she was looking for.

So she trailed out into the garden, hoping that one of the Smiths would be able to help her. The dew was heavy on the grass, and the sun had hardly started to come into the garden. Over on the Smiths' side there was complete silence. She called Joshua's name softly once or twice, but without any real hope of an answer. The only thing seemed to be to write a note. She went up into her sitting-room and tore out a page from her Greek exercise book. 'Can you come to the garden wall?' she wrote. 'I want to know where a place called Bodley is.' She folded the paper four times, and addressed it to Joshua. Thomas was far more likely to know, but she would never dare approach him on such a matter.

She opened the heavy door that opened into the college quad and marched briskly over to the porter's lodge. Nobody had ever said that she must not go out this way, though she had been warned by Mrs Clomper after the episode of the Jerusalem House dare that she might not go into the street alone without first asking permission.

'Could this note possibly be delivered to Professor Smith's house?' she said to the bowler-hatted Bastable who had chased her across the quad only two or three weeks ago. She hoped he had forgotten the incident by now. 'It's only just down the street,' she added pleadingly.

'Well, Miss, I think we might manage to go as far as that.' Bastable winked at one of his fellow porters. 'What do you say about it, Charlie? We wouldn't die of exhaustion, exactly, eh?'

And with that Maria had to be content. She returned to her sitting-room, and hung out of the window, waiting for a Smith to appear on the wall. It was some time before Joshua eventually did so, and then Maria rushed out to him. He let down the ladder, and looked furtively round, she clambered up it and down on to the Smiths' side.

'I thought you must have gone away,' she said as they went down to the bottom of the garden to sit under the apple trees. 'Why are you all so quiet?'

'Thomas is reading and won't lift his head out of his book, and James is patting a ball up and down and seeing how many bounces he can get. He keeps on trying to break his last record.'

'What is his record?'

'Seventy-six, so far.'

'What have you been doing, then?'

'Trying to write something about how you sail by the sun. I looked it up in Papa's *Encyclopaedia Britannica*, but I can't make out a single word of what it says there. It's always the same if I look something up in the encyclopaedia – either you can't understand a word, or else it tells you something completely different from what Mr Ledgard says, and anyway it's always far too long. There's a piece of news; Mr Ledgard's coming back, not this Monday but the next one.'

Maria's heart sank. The unknown was always frightening, and she had been hoping that perhaps Mr Ledgard's father would keep him away from Oxford at least until the holidays began. September and the autumn term were so far off that she did not much care what happened then. What would he think of her struggles with arithmetic and geometry? 'Is he very strict?' she asked.

'Stricter than Mr Copplestone. You have to work harder, and he doesn't take us out on expeditions like Mr Copplestone. But I think actually Papa is getting rather annoyed with Mr Copplestone. He says that the bull-fighting noise (only he doesn't know it's bull-fighting) is cracking the study ceiling.'

'Did anybody find out about James falling in the river?'

'Not yet. We've put all the wet things up in the attic, only we had to cover them up with dust sheets so that they wouldn't be seen, and it's awfully difficult to get things dry that way. But look, why are you writing notes about Bodley?'

'There was a man when I went down to dessert last night,' Maria explained, '(actually it was the man who pulled James out of the river), who spoke about a book being in Bodley, and it's a book I particularly wanted to read.'

'I expect he means the Bodleian Library then, where Papa and everybody go to read. Papa knows the librarian, the Protobibliotecarius Bodleianus, he calls him. We once played a game seeing how many words we could make out of Protobibliotecarius.'

'Can I go, then?' Maria asked doubtfully.

'Good heavens, no,' said Joshua, outraged. 'You have to belong to the University.'

'I suppose I could say I was Uncle Hadden's niece.'

'You just try saying you are. Go on, I dare you to.'

There was an appalled silence. 'Do you really dare me to?' said Maria weakly.

'Yes,' said Joshua, but very hesitantly.

'I'll have to try then, I suppose. Where is this library?'

'Do you know Broad Street? Well, then, you know those heads of the Roman emperors?'

'Those awful old statues without any noses on top of a wall?'

'They're not statues, they're only heads. Well, the Bodleian is next to that, back a bit from the road. I could take off the dare if you wanted.'

'No,' said Maria with determination. 'I'll do it.'

'Mrs Clomper,' she suggested nervously as they walked down Canterbury Lane a little later for their usual Saturday walk. 'Do you think we could go to the Bodleian Library? It's not very far away, and there would be time to go in the Parks afterwards.'

'But the Library's for gentlemen like your uncle, Miss Maria, not for little girls. Besides, now I come to think of it, I don't even know where it is.'

'I know where it is, it's only round the corner, in Broad Street, and please, I should very much like to see it.'

'Well, as long as it's not far, Miss Maria, we might go and look at the outside of it.'

Maria followed Joshua's directions, and they found themselves in a quadrangle surrounded by very old-looking buildings. There were a lot of doors with Latin inscriptions above.

'*Schola mathematica*,' read out Mrs Clomper, 'the mathematical school. You see, Miss Maria, I didn't require Latin lessons every day to be able to read a little Latin now and then. Good native wit, and *I* get by very well. Now, have you seen all you wanted to see?'

'I *should* like to go in,' said Maria, though she had not the least idea which of the doors led to the library.

Mrs Clomper was not really listening. 'Now, whatever can all that noise be in Broad Street? Is it those undergraduates at their tricks again? I really think we ought to go out this other way, Miss Maria, we don't want to get mixed up with any of those young men's junketings.'

There was certainly shouting and the thunder of approaching feet, which seemed to be coming rapidly nearer. Then a group of people burst into the quadrangle: 'Mad bull, mad bull!' they were shouting. 'Mad bull!' screamed Mrs Clomper, clutching at Maria with a tense arm, 'come quickly!' Maria rushed for the nearest door, Mrs Clomper hard on her heels. She struggled with the great iron latch, opened it, pulled Mrs Clomper in, and slammed the door shut. They were standing at the bottom of a staircase rather like the one in Jerusalem House, a staircase of shallow, uncarpeted steps, broken up by landings. 'Up the stairs, up the stairs!' moaned Mrs Clomper, and toiled up them ahead, disappearing round the first landing and up the second flight. 'Bulls climb stairs, come quickly, Miss Maria,' she called without turning round. But she had to halt from exhaustion on the second landing, and Maria, hurrying behind her, found her leaning against the wall with eyes closed, panting noisily.

There was a window there, fairly high in the wall, and Maria, standing on her toes, realized that the courtyard they had just left lay below them. Confused shouting and the sound of many feet scuffling in the gravel came up to her, and with a frantic effort she hoisted herself up by her hands to see what was going on. She had only had a second's glimpse of the scene below, but during that time she saw the flying feet and the tail of the bull disappearing under an archway out of the courtyard and men waving sticks in hot pursuit. She fell back on the floor. 'The bull, I saw the bull,' she shrieked. Mrs Clomper opened her eyes for a

She slowly slid down the wall

second, her head slumped forward on her chest, and she slowly slid down the wall until she was sitting on the floor in what seemed to be a dead faint.

It was an awkward situation, for there she was, sitting right in the way of anybody who might want to go up or down, and she really did look an alarming colour, blotchy mauve and white. Maria eyed her, aghast, and realized it was essential to find help. She made her way up the third flight of stairs, to be confronted with a glass-paned swing door, which said 'Silence' on it. Peering through the glass into the dim light beyond, Maria could see row upon row of books. She pushed her way boldly in; she was obviously in the Bodleian Library.

She expected to be pounced upon immediately by angry librarians demanding what she did there. But in fact there was nobody to be seen at all. She found herself in a dim, immensely high room lined with books. She walked forward, and found herself looking down into another part of the library. This had two lines of bookcases on either side of it, sticking out from the walls. She stood at the top and peered down its great length. There was nobody in sight, but the faint rustle of papers did indicate that there were people about. So she walked down to investigate.

There was indeed a considerable number of people working at tables on either side of the heavy black oak bookcases which divided up the room into a long series of recesses, but they were so grave and so intent on their work, that they hardly seemed human beings at all, and in spite of the grave emergency, with Mrs Clomper lying as dead outside, Maria felt it was out of the question to break into their concentration. She stole down towards the far end, peering into recess after recess, but not a head was raised. Pens scratched and pages were turned over, and sometimes there was a faint shuffle of feet below the desks, but otherwise there was silence. She came to the very end, and the last recess, and there was a man looking out of the window, thoughtfully biting his pen. She stood and watched him and he turned round sharply. Maria went up to him. 'A bull,' she said urgently, but remembering all the notices which said 'Silence', and 'Tread lightly and talk little'. 'And a lady has fainted.'

'A bull?' The man leant round the corner of the bookcase

and peered up the aisle. 'I don't see one,' he said with calm indifference.

'It isn't here,' whispered Maria, 'it's in the courtyard, or it was.'

'Then I don't think we need bother about it.' The man dipped his pen into the inkpot.

'But there's a lady outside who's fainted!' said Maria.

At that moment there were footsteps at the far end of the room. Maria's man craned round the bookcase again and made beckoning gestures. A young man with an immensely high forehead and receding fair hair that looked as though very soon it would slip right off the back of his head, advanced into view. He was carrying a pile of books. The man at the desk merely said, 'This young lady seems to be worried,' and bent his head over the papers in front of him. The whole episode was obviously wiped from his mind. The man with the high forehead raised his eyebrows.

'I came here to escape from a bull,' whispered Maria, with an instinct that this new arrival was probably one of the librarians.

'Oh?' said the young man. He shifted the books to his other arm, and still looked at Maria with querying eyebrows. She realized that the subject of the bull must be dropped, nobody in the Bodleian Library was in the slightest degree interested. 'The lady who was with me ran away from it and fainted,' she went on urgently. 'She's on the stairs now, what shall I do?'

'She must be moved if she's on the stairs.' The young man ran his fingers through his hair in a distracted way. 'Perhaps she would be well enough now to go downstairs,' he added hopefully. 'How long ago did it happen?'

'About five minutes. Perhaps you could help me take her downstairs,' said Maria.

It seemed to take him a long time to put his books down; Maria waited for him and shifted from one foot to another anxiously, worrying about Mrs Clomper, but afraid of going off by herself in case the young man disappeared. At last he was ready, and Maria ran ahead of him to the top of the stairs. When Maria had left her, Mrs Clomper had been slumped on the second landing, in the angle of the wall. But now she had gone.

'She's not there! Whatever can have happened?' said Maria with horror. 'Perhaps she got worse and rolled downstairs.' And she rushed on down. But Mrs Clomper was not on the second landing either. As Maria turned the last corner, a man just about to go out of the door at the bottom of the staircase turned round at the sound of the running footsteps. 'Have you seen a lady on these stairs who was rather ill?' she called.

He considered. 'I did see a lady a moment or so ago being assisted downstairs by a gentleman who was talking of finding her a cab. A middle-aged lady in purple. Would she be the one you were inquiring for?'

'Oh, thank you, yes,' and Maria ran upstairs to tell the young man. But when she reached the top he too had gone. 'I suppose that as soon as he saw that poor Mrs Clomper's corpse wasn't blocking the stairs he didn't care any more,' Maria thought to herself. She peered through the glass of the swing door, and felt that she hardly dared disturb him again just to tell him that Mrs Clomper in fact did seem to have recovered. Unless, now that she was in Bodley itself, she went to ask him whether he could find her that book on the Fitzackerleys. If he took the news about the mad bull so calmly, he ought to be calmer still when he was asked for a book. So, for a second time, she walked into the dim light of the library.

She made out the young man, sitting at a desk in the

distance and scribbling away furiously, as though to make up for the time he had wasted with her. She presented herself at his desk. 'I wonder if you could very kindly find me a book?' she asked politely.

This request had the most astonishing effect on the young man. He dropped his pencil and stared at her, his eyebrows nearly in his hair. 'A book?' he said at last. 'You want a book?'

Maria tried to explain. 'A Mr Benson told me that there was a book about the Fitzackerley family in the seventeenth century in Bodley. I don't know if I would be allowed to read it here. I don't belong to the University,' she told him, remembering what Joshua had said. 'But my uncle is the Warden of Canterbury College.' And she then added as an afterthought, 'Are you the Protobibliotecarius Bodleianus?'

'No,' said the young man with a gasp. 'Would you like to see him?'

'Oh, no,' said Maria, 'I don't think so, thank you.'

But the young man had risen hurriedly. 'His room is this way, if you will just follow me.' He led the way, up a small staircase. Maria had to run to keep up with him; she was far too appalled at what she had brought upon herself to notice where she was being led. He stopped in front of a heavy oak door, which had painted above it the ominous words, 'Protobibliotecarius Bodleianus'. He knocked, put his head in for a moment to say, 'The niece of the Warden of Canterbury College to see the Librarian.' And with that brief introduction he pushed Maria into the room.

The Librarian was an exceedingly thin man with tight lips and gold pince-nez. He got up from his desk as Maria came into the room, and stood there forbiddingly, his arms folded against his waistcoat.

'I only wondered whether I could read one of your books,'

said Maria with great nervousness. 'I didn't really want to disturb you, and it doesn't matter if I can't.'

'You are not, I take it, a member of this University,' said the Librarian.

'No,' said Maria, 'though my uncle is.'

'This is a most unheard of request,' said the Librarian, 'and I should like to make it clear that I disapprove of women in the University.'

'Yes,' said Maria meekly.

'But nevertheless,' continued the Librarian, 'since you are the Warden's niece, and he and I are of the same mind about women in the University . . .'

'Oh, but . . .' said Maria anxiously, feeling it was only fair to correct the Librarian over this. He gave her a quelling look. 'Since, as I say, Warden Henniker-Hadden and I are in agreement over this matter, and he presumably countenanced this visit of yours . . .' Maria again tried to correct him, 'I don't think . . .' she began, but the Librarian paid no attention. '. . . I will give my permission for you to consult this book.' He strode towards the door. Maria hesitated, and then decided she was supposed to follow him. The Librarian walked on ahead of her to where the fair-haired young man was sitting. He was still scribbling furiously, and turned round with a startled expression as the Librarian approached him. 'Mr Evans,' said the Librarian, 'will you be kind enough to administer the oath to Miss Henniker-Hadden and find her the book she requires.' He stalked away. Mr Evans looked at Maria with such astonishment that she dropped her eyes to the floor with confusion. Then he thrust something across the desk to her. 'Will you read this aloud, please,' he said.

Maria looked at the piece of card, and began to read aloud the solemn oath that it had printed on it that she would not damage or steal anything belonging to the Library. Her voice sounded unnaturally loud in the stillness; surely Mr Evans had never intended her to read it aloud in a room where you had to be silent? By the time she came to the promise not to 'kindle therein any fire or flame' she was certain that he had meant her to read it to herself and broke off abruptly. He did not seem to notice, but pushed a huge register towards her. 'Will you sign this, please,' he said. 'Now, what book is it that you want?'

'It was a book about the Fitzackerley family in the seventeenth century,' Maria repeated. He pushed back his chair, and once again she followed him, up the stairs, across wastes of floor where their footsteps crashed noisily. He stopped in front of shelves, about a hundred yards of them, bearing vast volumes that all looked the same.

'Is this it?' asked Maria timidly as he pulled out one of them.

'This is the catalogue of the Library,' Mr Evans said cuttingly, turning over pages very rapidly. 'Fitzabbot, Fitzackerley. Did you say the name was Fitzackerley? Very well, this must be the book: *An Account of the Lives of some Members of the Family of Fitzackerley*.'

'Yes, I think so,' said Maria, who had really no more idea than Mr Evans about the title of the book. He copied it down on a piece of paper. 'I'll get it fetched for you. You had better go and sit down in Duke Humphrey until it comes.'

'In Duke Humphrey?' Maria repeated, bewildered.

'I'll take you.' And back they marched again over the long floors.

Duke Humphrey turned out to be the long library with the rows of recesses partitioned off by bookcases, and Mr Evans left her there. She sat at the far end of one of the recesses, by a tall window that reached almost to the ground, and thought about her tremendous daring. As for Mrs

Clomper – Maria had done her best, and if that lady just abandoned her, she must expect a little delay in being rejoined.

But by the time they brought her the book she was feeling rather frightened at what was going to happen to her when she got back to the Lodgings. And she hardly dared open the book after all the oaths she had just sworn not to damage it. Fingering the corners only, she turned over the first few pages with great delicacy, and came almost at once to the family tree. It was set out on a huge sheet of paper folded into the book. Maria spread it out like a tablecloth and pored over it. She hit upon the name she wanted almost at once; Stephen St George Fitzackerley, only son of Richard, ninth Lord Fitzackerley, born in 1640, but the date of his death was unknown. And he had one sister, Deborah, who had died when she was ten. It all fitted in with her ideas, and it meant that S. St G. F. had been fourteen years old when he carved 'Begone, ye foul traitors' with such ferocity in the stone at Jerusalem House. Now, if only she could find out something about the life of this Stephen, and the reason why he carved those words, it would surely be a very interesting piece of research.

Thoroughly excited, her hands almost trembling, she turned over the pages to see what was said in the chapter on the ninth Lord Fitzackerley. There were some fifty pages on him, which she began to read, hoping to find references to his children. But what with her excitement, and a guilty feeling that she ought to go back and show herself to Mrs Clomper, she realized that she was not doing it justice. The only thing was to come back again with a paper and pencil, and give up a whole afternoon to reading and making notes.

Very reluctantly she closed the book and took it back to Mr Evans, half afraid that by letting it go now she would never see it again. But Mr Evans had gone, perhaps to his lunch, and after waiting a moment in case he returned, she left it on his desk. Outside the Bodleian quadrangle had returned to its usual calm, and looking at its sunny emptiness nobody could possibly tell that a mad bull had raged through it half an hour before. Or was it an hour ago? or even two hours? In the Bodleian one did not notice passing time, just as one did not notice mad bulls, and realizing that the whole morning might have gone while she was there, Maria broke into a run.

She was just turning breathlessly into Canterbury Lane when out shot the three Smiths, pounding along like steam engines. 'Bastable says there's a mad bull,' shouted Thomas, 'and old Copplestone is trying to bull-fight it.'

'Oh, Thos,' shrieked James, 'do come on or we'll miss them.'

Maria watched them charging away down the street, and then chased after them. 'Where are you going?' she panted, as she drew alongside Joshua, the slowest of the three.

'Bastable says he saw them in St Giles, and Mr Copplestone trying to attract the bull's attention with a policeman's cape. Thos, do wait, I've got an awful stitch.'

But Thomas and James ran on until they had stitches too, and panting and heaving, had to slow down. They were now in the broad tree-lined road of St Giles, but the street was empty of any bull-fights.

'I saw the bull too,' said Maria, gasping for breath. 'It came rushing through the Bodleian Library. It frightened Mrs Clomper into a dead faint.'

'Through the Bodleian!' shrieked Thomas. 'Great heavens; talk about a bull in a china shop! That ought to stir up all the old Bodley buffers.'

'Oh, not in the library, in the quad outside. But that was ages ago, fancy them still not being able to catch the bull.'

They were now at a standstill. There was not a sign of

the bull or of Mr Copplestone. 'They have probably caught it now,' said Thomas gloomily. 'We only got the news second-hand from Bastable.' A group of men were coming up a side street towards them. Thomas went up to them. 'Excuse me, but do you know if the bull has been caught?' he asked.

'Just trying to shoot him now, down by the canal,' one of the men shouted. 'Got him cornered at last.'

'Come on, then, we must see,' shouted James, and he ran on down the side street in the direction the men had come from. The others had to follow. 'Thos,' wailed Joshua, 'we don't want to see them shooting.'

'Go home then,' he called over his shoulder. They had turned out of the side street now, into Walton Street, the road that ran parallel to St Giles, and the high pillars of the University Press buildings were in sight. As they drew level with the entrance, the sound of raised, excited voices from the garden of the Press attracted their attention, and they stopped.

'It's the Streak,' called James, and with that bolted under the archway that gave on to the garden quadrangle of the University Press.

There he was, Mr Copplestone, standing waist deep in the pond in the middle of the lawn, surrounded with angry men who seemed to be trying to order him out.

'No, no, my good sir,' Mr Copplestone was saying amiably as they came up. 'Until you can assure me that the bull is as dead as mutton (or shall we say beef), or at least penned in, I must refuse to leave the safety of your pond, uncomfortable and uncleanly as it is.'

'But the bull has gone, sir, do you hear?' said the angriest of the men; he had white hair and a white moustache. 'And meanwhile you are trespassing and causing damage to Press property.'

'But consider the damage that the bull would cause to me,' argued Mr Copplestone, 'and even the Press would hardly like to have the death of a clergyman on its hands.'

'Theatrical nonsense,' said the white-haired man.

Mr Copplestone wagged his finger from the middle of the pond. 'I know the ways of bulls, if I may say so, sir, and you do not. A bull, once engaged in contest by a matador, will not give in until he has killed the matador, or the matador has killed him. I am that matador, and I must continue to take refuge in your pond.'

'Go in and fetch him out,' said the white-haired man to a printing hand who was standing by in oily overalls. 'Fetch him out, do you hear me?'

'Not me, sir, can't swim, sir,' said the hand backing hastily away.

'Swim!' said the man contemptuously. 'You haven't got to swim. However ...' And he began to strip off his coat.

'They're going to fight in the pond,' shrieked James, who was rolling on the grass in ecstasy at this scene. 'Oh, tell them to stop being so funny. I'm hurting with so much laughing.' At that moment there was the sudden sound of two gunshots from the direction of the canal. 'That's him,' said one of the men standing at the pond's edge. 'Killed him at last.'

'Finis,' said Mr Copplestone. 'Farewell to a noble animal, who made a bold bid for life.' And he swept off his hat and bowed his head. 'And now, sir, I am indeed glad to tell you that I can leave this pond.'

CHAPTER TEN

Mr Copplestone's Assistance

THE astonishing thing about that Saturday morning was Mrs Clomper's behaviour afterwards. Maria returned to the Lodgings, excited, wildly untidy, without the least idea of the time, and with no excuses to explain her long absence. She found Mrs Clomper in a state of nervous prostration, certain that Maria must have been gored by the bull or trampled on by the mob, all through having been abandoned in the Bodleian. 'I felt so poorly that I just did not know what I was doing,' she kept saying. 'And when a gentlemen came along and took me downstairs and offered to find me a cab I forgot everything else but how ill I was feeling.' Maria guiltily protested that of course it did not matter, and that she soon found out what had happened. But Mrs Clomper still felt that she had failed in her duty, and failed the Warden, and that it would have been entirely her fault if Maria had never come back to the Lodgings.

'I shouldn't allow her to forget that,' said Thomas when Maria told him how affairs had turned out. 'If you can manage to keep her feeling guilty, it might make her more kindly towards you for life.'

'How can I keep her feeling guilty?'

'Just by behaving in a pathetic, lost, meek way, I should think. I must say that for a girl who is so mouselike by nature, you do some pretty startling things – storming Bodley for instance.'

This praise pleased Maria enormously, and she put it down in her diary. Thomas and Joshua were the only people whom she had told about her adventure in the Bodleian, and she had sworn them to secrecy, and hoped that the library officials would not talk to her uncle. But the difficulty was going to be to return to the library with time enough to read the book; she was hungry to do more research, and to find out more facts.

'Why don't you go tomorrow afternoon?' Joshua suggested. 'There aren't going to be any lessons because Mamma is giving a croquet party and we've got to be there. I can't think why.'

'It's to hand round things at tea-time,' said James, 'and to help the lady-students play croquet.'

'Lady-students?' queried Maria.

'The party is chiefly for Papa's lady-students,' said Joshua, 'he's very interested in them.'

'Then the Protobibliotecarius wouldn't get on well with him,' said Maria. 'He disapproves of women in the university, and disapproves of people approving of them.'

'Papa and he detest each other,' said Thomas lazily.

This was Monday evening, after tea, and they were sunning themselves under the apple trees in the Smiths' garden before they went in to do their homework. Thomas threw baby apples in an indolent way at the cat, who was washing himself in a patch of sun near the house. 'Papa has just heard about Mr Copplestone and the bull,' he announced. 'Joshua wouldn't let anybody tell him on Saturday, though I can't think why we agreed to it.'

'However did you stop Jas from telling?' Maria asked.

'Jos told him that Papa would stop us bull-fighting in the schoolroom. That kept him quiet – though he kept spluttering all through lunch.'

'It was so funny, Mr Copplestone in that pond, and all the people so angry with him.' James began laughing again as he thought of it.

'Papa's angry too. I heard him telling Mamma that the man was a menace to all our sanity.'

'Does he mean the sanity of us three and Maria?' Joshua asked.

'He's threatening my sanity, anyway,' said Thomas. 'I don't know that the rest of you have much to lose. I can't tell you how thankful I am that Mr Ledgard is coming back next week.'

'We might as well have told Papa on Saturday now that he knows anyway,' said James mournfully. 'I was so longing to. And the Streak said he is never going to bull-fight again. I asked him. He said he was so upset by the bull paying no attention to what he did with the policeman's cape.'

'The bull was mad,' said Joshua. 'In Spain, bull-fighters don't have to face mad bulls.'

'I thought all bulls were mad,' said Maria. 'I mean, that you said they were, whether they were mad or sane.'

' "Mad, bad, and dangerous to know",' quoted Thomas, 'Like the Reverend Francis Copplestone.'

'He's not bad,' said Joshua indignantly.

'But you can't deny he's the other things. Do you suppose Mamma will provide a good tea for her croquet party?'

'Cucumber sandwiches, anyway,' said James. 'I asked Cook.'

'Oh, no!' said Joshua with horror. 'How awful, and you can never tell that they're cucumber until you take a bite and then it's too late.'

'You can spit it out,' James suggested.

'You hardly ever can, unless you hold it in your mouth for ages. And anyway, it's the feel of the cucumber more than anything else.'

'Do you think that anyone would see me if I got up the pear tree?' Maria asked. 'I want to see what the lady-students are like.'

'Terrible,' said Thomas.

'In what way terrible?'

'They're rather knobbly and they wear spectacles,' said Joshua. 'The proper undergraduates are all right, they play cricket with us. But the lady-students . . . oh, I don't know. You'll be one yourself one day.'

'Yes, so she will, I'd forgotten that. Yes, Maria, you had better get up that tree and see for yourself what you must avoid,' ordered Thomas.

'All right, I will, and I'll make faces at you and try and make you laugh.'

'I hope you can make Thos laugh,' said Joshua. 'He's usually so cross at Mamma's parties that he won't say a word to anybody.'

'I'll only be there a little of the time, because I want to go and read some more of the book. But you don't think your mother and father will be able to see me?'

'I shouldn't think they'll bother to look farther than the croquet lawn,' Joshua assured her.

The next afternoon she was up in the tree long before she need have been, and began to feel bruised by the knobbles. She could hear James's voice occasionally raised in high-pitched protests. They were evidently putting him into his best sailor suit. Presently he wandered out. She was pleased that he did not notice her, it meant that she was reasonably well hidden. He was dragging a stick noisily against the rose trellis, and muttering, 'Silly old lady-students, silly old lady-students.' Inside the house Mrs Smith could be heard talking at a breathless rate. Then Thomas and Joshua appeared. Thomas held a book in his hand and seemed to be absorbed in it. Maria suspected it was all pretence. 'What's Thos reading?' she called.

Joshua looked up at the pear tree and came over. 'It's Greek – Herodotus. It's all show really because he can hardly make out what a single word means. But he wants to show the lady-students that he's cleverer than they are. He despises them dreadfully.' They looked at Thomas, who sat down in one of the garden chairs and turned over a page in a self-conscious way.

'Yes, I thought he didn't look as if he was really reading. Could you see me up here before I called? Because if I'm very obvious I had better get down.'

'No, you're all right unless anybody stands right below. I wish I was up there. I do hate meeting new people. Oh, dear, I can hear voices in the hall. I suppose they're coming.'

Three young women came down the steps into the garden and stood in a nervous huddle eyeing the boys. Thomas put his finger in his book, closed it, and wandered over in a lordly way to do his duty. But at this point Professor Smith bustled out. 'My son, Thomas,' Maria heard him say breezily. 'Thomas, you must take note of these young ladies. You'll probably find that when you reach the university you'll be attending their lectures.' There was a nervous titter, and then the boldest of them began to chatter to the professor; the others stood in silence, and watched her enviously. More lady-students arrived, and a sprinkling of men. Then, surprisingly, came Mr Copplestone. He stood with bent head at the foot of the steps by the garden door, and smiled at his shoes. Why, he's as shy as Joshua, thought Maria. Joshua was hovering at the edge of a chattering group of women, watching their faces as they talked, too nervous to speak himself, and too nervous to move away. Then Mrs Smith began to arrange croquet quartets. Mr Copplestone backed farther and farther away. Maria watched him with interest, thinking that he would never be able to avoid Mrs Smith's eye. But he did. He drifted out of the proceedings until he was standing under the pear tree, directly below

Maria, and watching the croquet groups with great attention.

'My spies tell me that you are reading at the Bodleian,' Maria suddenly heard him say. 'May I ask if you are conducting some research of your own?' He had not moved his head at all, his eyes seemed to be glued on the croquet, but there was no one else near him, and he must have been speaking to her. She was very confused. Apart from anything else, it was so embarrassing being discovered peeping, but frightened in case he repeated the question in a louder voice, she made a rustling noise to show she had heard. 'I can't tell you from here,' she whispered, pushing her head low through the branches.

Mr Copplestone looked up for an instant. 'Oh, but you can. Look how far we are from the battleground. And they are all taking the croquet so seriously. Besides, you know what a curious nature I have, and you can't let me spend another sleepless night wondering about it, can you now?'

Maria knew Mr Copplestone well enough by this time to realize that unless she satisfied him he would not go away. So with much rustling and swaying of the tree which she hoped was not being noticed from the croquet lawn, she lay full length on her front and whispered down at him in short hisses. 'I was wanting to find out something about Jerusalem House.'

'Ha,' said Mr Copplestone quite loudly, screwing his head round to look at her. 'It was that drawing of an unknown boy that inspired you, was it? And have you made any progress?'

'Not very much,' said Maria.

Silence fell again. From the lawn came the click of croquet mallets and voices raised in despair and apology as the ball failed to do what was required of it. Through the leaves

Maria could see Professor Smith watching the game with a young woman in spectacles and the three boys. His voice boomed across to her. 'If I can presume to give you some advice, my dear young lady, never accept a man's offer of marriage until you have played a game of croquet with him. Croquet is quite unequalled for showing up a person's character. If he is bad-tempered or inclined to cheat it will all come out, you know.'

'Is that how you chose Mamma?' James's voice was as penetrating as his father's.

'Oh, no, my dear boy. Croquet would have been quite useless with your mamma, because if she tries to hit a ball it nearly always goes backwards, and a game would have shown up my bad temper, not hers.'

'It was really something else at the house that I was interested in,' whispered Maria.

Mr Copplestone looked up again. 'You had better come down from that tree of yours and we'll discuss the matter further.'

'I can't. I haven't been asked to the party.'

'Very well, then. I must come in to you.' Mr Copplestone surveyed the croquet party doubtfully. 'But I don't think I can get over the wall today. Or do you think I can?'

'Oh, no,' said Maria, terrified that he might try. 'I think you had better go round. I'll let you in through the gate from the college garden. Perhaps if you went out of this garden by the tradesmen's entrance? Then you wouldn't have to go through their hall.' She watched him wander in a zig-zag way up the path, his hands clasped behind his back. Then she slid down the tree. She had to wait a long time at the gate at the other side of the garden. She could see him sniffing at the roses in the college gardens through the gate. 'A fine display of roses Canterbury is going to have this year,' he remarked cheerfully as Maria let him in. 'Now, tell me what other line of research you are pursuing at Jerusalem House?'

So Maria told him about the inscription and the initials and how she had linked them with the picture of the little boy and his sister. 'At first I did want to find out who the "unknown boy" was,' she finished up, 'but I didn't know how to start.'

'Oh, I could very probably throw some light on that,' said Mr Copplestone confidently. 'At least, I could tell you the date of the drawing if I saw it. Why shouldn't we set out for Jerusalem House?'

Maria was stupefied. 'Go to Jerusalem House?' she said feebly.

'I think I am capable of taking myself to Jerusalem House,' said Mr Copplestone offended. 'It doesn't seem to need any great intellect. Shall we go now?'

'What, now?'

'An excellent time, I should think. The three young Smiths are occupied and can't trouble us. You say we can get in by the garden gate if we go round the wall – so what is there to stop us?'

'But what about Mrs Clomper?'

'Surely an excursion with one's tutor is a good enough reason for any woman?'

'But I can't interrupt her, she's having a friend from Bicester to tea,' wailed Maria.

'Bicester? Yes, that is a long way to come to tea. Very well, go and tell the Warden then. We must hurry because I am dining out tonight.'

Maria felt she could argue no longer. She trotted miserably up the gravel to the garden door. There was no answer to her knock on the study door. She pushed it open, and peered cautiously in. The room was empty and a fly buzzed and bumped against the window. She ran softly upstairs and seized her hat, and then when she repassed Mrs Clomper's room she hesitated outside. There was a sound of voices inside, she could not possibly disturb Mrs Clomper. She went downstairs. She could not keep Mr Copplestone waiting much longer, but what was she to do? The grandfather clock in the hall loudly ticked away the seconds as she hesitated there. There were footsteps from the kitchen passage, and Lizzie appeared with a trayload of freshly cleaned silver candlesticks on her way to the dining-room. 'Oh, Lizzie,' said Maria. Lizzie stopped dead and looked at her nervously. 'If anyone wants me I've had to go out with Mr Copplestone. Only don't bother to tell anybody unless they ask.' She rushed off; it was a relief that somebody in the house knew where she was.

Once in St Giles, Mr Copplestone hailed a hansom and bundled Maria into it. 'Drive to Long Slinfold, my man,' he told the cabby, 'and you'll be well rewarded.'

'Long Slinfold?' said the man, rubbing his nose and looking Mr Copplestone up and down with great curiosity. 'That's a tidy step, guv'nor. Still, you're the loser, and George and me won't say no to a nice little jaunt in the country. Hop in, then. Hup, George!' And George set off at a smart trot.

'It's to save time, you know,' said Mr Copplestone, sinking back against the musty cushions. 'Don't you think it's a good idea?' But Maria's thoughts were on Mrs Clomper, and whether the sister-in-law from Bicester would take up her attention for long enough for her not to notice Maria's absence.

'It's not Friday,' she said dismally. 'How are we going to get in?'

'By the same method, presumably, as you have just told me that you and the young Smiths forced an entrance a few days ago.'

'But we didn't go into the house.'

'We'll see what can be done about that when we get there. Meantime, we could always look at your inscription.'

But her gloom did lift presently, and she watched the passing country with interest. The horse, George, clopped along much faster than Uncle Matt's grey mare, and the windows were rather dirty, but even so she recognized most of the road, and became quite excited at the thought of taking her research a stage further. Presently they came to that wooded stretch that she remembered from their previous expedition. Mr Copplestone opened the little window in the roof that communicated with the cabby. 'We are just approaching Jerusalem House,' he called up. 'I want you to drive us up the avenue.'

'Cor,' said the cabby. 'Toffs, ain't you!'

But there was still the lodgekeeper to deal with. The cab slowed down before the massive iron gates. The lodge-keeper was in his garden again, leaning on his spade, surrounded by two or three gaping, tow-haired children. Mr Copplestone leaned out. 'Good afternoon, my man, and how's your good wife?'

'Bad,' said the lodgekeeper briefly.

'Sorry to hear it, sorry to hear it. Here's something for you to buy sugar mice for those fine children of yours. And now would you open the gates for us like a good fellow, we are in a hurry to reach the house. We'll be back again very shortly, so don't trouble to shut them.'

Maria marvelled at the way grown-ups seemed to get what they wanted without the least trouble, and not even a warning about racketing about the woods. 'But how did you know he had a wife?' she asked.

'Have you ever known a lodgekeeper without a wife?' said Mr Copplestone. He seemed in high spirits and hummed loudly. The road was rougher in the avenue, and the cab moved more slowly. It was five minutes before the great wall with the gatehouse towering in the middle appeared between the trees. The cab drew up.

'Strikes me you're going to need gunpowder to get in, not a visiting card,' said the cabby, eyeing the massive door, and chuckling hoarsely at his wit.

'Ah, we are more privileged,' said Mr Copplestone clambering out. 'We use a private entrance. We shall not be longer than three-quarters of an hour, if you will be so good as to wait for us. Here is a little pamphlet of my own composition for you to read in the meantime. It deals with the cultivation of fig trees in ancient Babylonia.'

Maria pointed towards the left, and they hurried down the lane under the wall, Maria taking jerky little runs to keep up with Mr Copplestone's long strides. They looked back at the cabby before they turned the corner. He had his pipe stuck in his mouth and was staring at the sky, while George was nibbling peacefully at the grass verge. Maria felt full of alarm at what lay ahead. Disasters always seemed to fall round Mr Copplestone like autumn leaves, and what might happen this time when he was deliberately walking into danger was too horrible to contemplate. Her only hope was that the garden gate might be locked this time.

But when they reached the gate it was still slightly ajar. They squeezed in, and there they were, standing in the old orchard, where the overgrown apple trees shut out most of the light. Maria led the way over to the gate in the wall that opened into the gardens. Mr Copplestone rustled through the grass behind, beating the twigs from his face. When they arrived in the garden that held the fantastically shaped yew bushes Maria conducted him over the lawn, creeping from the protection of one tree to the next, listening furtively for gardeners. They climbed the steps into the garden where the little box hedges swept in scrolls and curves. 'The inscription is on the bottom of the parapet over there,' whispered Maria, pointing to the flight of steps beyond that led up on to the terrace.

'Very well,' said Mr Copplestone briskly, 'I will now proceed to make a drawing of it. Stay here if you are nervous.'

The next five minutes were agonizing. With the utmost calm Mr Copplestone knelt at the bottom of the steps carefully making an exact copy as though he had all the time in the world. At last he painfully pulled himself up and brushed the gravel off his trousers. 'I have no sensation in either knee,' he called out. Maria poked her head out from behind a bush and looked at him beseechingly. But Mr Copplestone took no notice; he went on dusting himself down, the whole enormous length of him, standing brazenly in full view of the myriads of windows in the house above. When this was finished, he turned round to look at the house. 'Alas, alas,' he mused, 'all those windows veiled in yellow blinds by Miss Hickmott. How one longs to wrench them all up and let sun and life into the place!' And with that, he started to move up the steps. For a second Maria watched him, and then she darted out from shelter and caught him up. 'We can't go up there,' she said in a voice squeaky with agitation. 'And anyway the cab is waiting for us.'

'And can continue to wait,' said Mr Copplestone. 'For after all the man will be liberally paid for it. And George is in a horse's paradise. No, I want to examine this garden façade of the house more closely than Miss Hickmott allowed us to do before.' He was now on the terrace and walking with measured tread over the grass. The house was completely still. Mr Copplestone marched straight towards the door and laid his hand on it. It opened. He looked back at Maria and made a clucking sound of disapproval. 'How careless of Miss Hickmott!' And in he went.

Maria followed, limp with terror, and there they both stood, trespassers in Jerusalem House, in the stone passage that smelt like a church. Mr Copplestone did not trouble to listen for approaching footsteps. He went boldly on, through the doorway in the high oak screen into the hall. They climbed the staircase, making a great deal of noise. 'Now where was this drawing?' Mr Copplestone asked.

Maria pointed to the room at the top of the stairs which Miss Hickmott had called Lady Margaret's Gallery. 'Undoubtedly a drawing by Lely, said Mr Copplestone when he reached the picture, 'you can accept that with the utmost confidence. And the boy is probably a Fitzackerley, as Thomas said. He is wearing a curious little chain which ought to help you identify him.'

Maria had not noticed it before. She stood on tiptoe to peer up at the boy who looked down at her with his heavy-lidded eyes. 'I'm sure the little boy in the other picture had a gold chain something like that.' She ran to see, and Mr Copplestone followed. 'You know,' he said, tapping at the picture with his forefinger, 'I should say that the little Stephen Fitzackerley in this picture and our friend in the drawing were one and the same boy. The probable date of the paintings, the resemblance, the chain, everything points to it.'

But Maria was not listening to him. She was straining to hear a faint sound. 'I'm sure I can hear something,' she said, clutching Mr Copplestone's arm. 'Yes, I can; listen.' From the distance, but rapidly approaching, came the clatter of several footsteps on wooden floors. 'We'll have to hide,' she said, looking wildly round her.

'We shall do no such thing,' said Mr Copplestone. 'Who am I if I cannot deal with a thousand Miss Hickmotts?'

She was on them now, coming through the door like a tug-boat with a stream of small barges behind her, a man, a woman, and two small boys in sailor suits clutching hats. But as she was speaking to them over her shoulder it was not she who first noticed the intruders. 'Auntie!' shrilled one of the small boys. 'Here's burglars!'

'Miss Hickmott,' said Mr Copplestone stepping forward. 'How very pleasant to see you. Now we shall be able to pay you our joint two shillings for the privilege of being admitted.'

'Well, I never did,' panted Miss Hickmott, falling back and clutching her dress front. 'You audacious man!' As she seemed too overcome to go on, the man took over. He looked as though he might be her brother. 'You could be put in prison for this,' he said grimly. 'Housebreaking, that's what the magistrates call it. And frightening the ladies like this, you might easily have two deaths on your hands. And that'd be murder. What have you got to say for yourself, hey?'

'My profound apologies, of course, for upsetting the ladies,' said Mr Copplestone hanging his head in the way that was so familiar to Maria. 'But you can hardly call it housebreaking when I offer you our entrance money. As a matter of fact we came in a perfectly decent manner. We drove up the main entrance in a cab.'

'Giraffe!' exploded Miss Hickmott, to everyone's astonishment. She then became speechless with anger again. Maria wondered if they had frightened her into a sort of fit.

'And a gentleman of your profession too, dragging a poor innocent child into this!' continued the man. The two little boys stared open-mouthed at them both.

'Innocent!' said Miss Hickmott with difficulty. 'Innocent! Young limb of Satan, that's what I say.'

Maria felt on the verge of tears. 'We're very sorry,' she said thickly. 'May we go now?'

Mr Copplestone was fumbling in his pocket. 'Allow me to give you my card,' he said brightly. 'And then if you find a Van Dyck is missing you can get in touch with me.'

Miss Hickmott sat down heavily in one of the armchairs shrouded in its holland cover. But she seemed to be recovering. 'Albert,' she said. 'Here are the keys. Take them out, if you please, by the side courtyard, and don't rest until you've bolted and barred the gates behind them. It wouldn't surprise me if he wasn't a dangerous lunatic. Elsie, do you happen to have your smelling salts about you? I've come over quite queer.'

Maria and Mr Copplestone trailed down the stairs behind Miss Hickmott's brother, who kept his head over his shoulder watching them the whole way. He led them along dark stone passages.

'Aha, the domestic offices,' said Mr Copplestone happily. 'I have never been privileged to see this part of the house before.' He peered in at the doors they passed.

'Come along out of that,' said Miss Hickmott's brother. 'We want you out of this house quick.' He rattled his keys menacingly.

Soon they were standing in a courtyard where grass grew in tufts between the stones and pigeons strutted and cooed. 'We will not trouble you to call our carriage,' said Mr Copplestone with a sweet smile. 'It is just round by the gatehouse entrance, and we can easily walk.'

Miss Hickmott's brother could find nothing to say to this, and had to content himself with furious mutterings as he slammed the courtyard gate at Mr Copplestone's heels. George was still cropping the grass when they turned the corner, and the cabby was lolling back with his eyes fixed glassily on the sky. Mr Copplestone's pamphlet was lying unopened on his knee. He did not take his eyes off the sky until they were within touching distance of the cab. Then

'Elsie, do you happen to have your smelling salts about you?'

he gathered up the reins. 'I hope the dook was in good health, and his lady too,' and he gave a great guffaw of laughter.

'We will return to Oxford now,' said Mr Copplestone. 'We have spent a very interesting afternoon, and I hope that you and your good animal are well rested.'

'I don't know about that,' said the cabby. 'But we wants our tea, don't we, George?' He drove off and the cab lurched from side to side as they went down the avenue. Maria stared out of the window and hoped that Mr Copplestone was not going to talk to her. But he hummed loudly and wrote things in his pocket book. The dusty road and the hedges gave way to gardens and houses here and there and then they were in Oxford.

'Twenty-five minutes past five,' said Mr Copplestone, peering at his watch. 'I wonder if my absence from the croquet has been remarked upon?' Maria felt certain that James would have pointed it out to the whole party two minutes after Mr Copplestone had left, but she said nothing.

'Such a remarkable afternoon,' said Mr Copplestone as he unfolded himself from the cab in St Giles. Maria stood beside him as he counted out the fare with great thoroughness. She looked anxiously up and down the street, and horrors, here was the Bishop in his apron and gaiters and strings on his top hat, sailing towards them. She looked at Mr Copplestone. He was laboriously counting out sixpences into the cabby's hand, and every now and then forgetting how many he had handed over, and having to start again. The Bishop had not marked her down yet, he was looking at Mr Copplestone's great height as though he knew it well. Maria felt she could not face meeting him and the questions that would be asked. She said hastily, 'If you will excuse me, Mr Copplestone, I really think I ought to go home in case they want me. Thank you for taking me to the house.'

And she set off without waiting for an answer. She heard her tutor give a bay of delight as he recognized the Bishop. 'A-ah, my lord. I have spent such an interesting afternoon . . .' But at this she took to her heels and ran; she could not bear to think what Mr Copplestone was about to blurt out to the Bishop. As she turned off St Giles she looked back for a second. There was Mr Copplestone standing by the cab, and there was the Bishop hurrying away from him, almost at a run.

CHAPTER ELEVEN

More Embarrassment at Bodley

'Maria,' said Thomas when she came in for lessons the next morning, 'just what were you and the Streak up to yesterday afternoon? You both disappeared in a very shifty way. Did you take him to the Bodleian, or did he take you?'

Maria shuddered at the memory of yesterday afternoon. 'No, we didn't go there. It was awful. It was the worst afternoon I have ever spent in my life. I could never have believed that anything could be so embarrassing.'

'But what *happened*?' they all shouted at her.

'Papa was telling Mamma that he saw the Bishop last night,' said Joshua, 'and the Bishop said that the Streak had gone up to him in St Giles and carried on alarming about the awfulness of unmarried women; he was quite frightened – the Bishop, I mean.'

'But was what the Streak said anything to do with what you did that afternoon?' urged Thomas. 'We could hardly go to sleep last night for wondering. Did you have a battle with Mrs Clomper or something? No, of course, she's not unmarried. What *did* you do?'

So Maria told them. 'It was agony, every single second of it,' she finished. 'The only thing was that nobody at the Lodgings seemed to know that I had been away all afternoon. And now Miss Hickmott has got the Streak's card, and so she'll be able to track us down.'

'Did you find anything out from the pictures?' Joshua asked.

'Yes, I had forgotten about that. It was an extraordinary

thing, the Streak thinks that the unknown boy is Stephen Fitzackerley, the little boy in the picture with his sister, and the boy that I think carved those words on the parapet. What I'd really like to find out now is what made him carve them. If only I could get back and read that book in the Bodleian!'

'You had better go on Friday, hadn't you,' said Thomas. 'It will be our last Copplestone day, and you'll never manage anything with Mr Ledgard around, he's like a hawk. Cut Friday afternoon's lessons and go along. Go on, you've done so many frightful things the last fortnight that one more won't make any difference.'

'Anyway,' said James airily, 'the Streak probably can't count. Birds can't, you know. If there are four eggs and you take away one they don't know.'

'I expect Mr Copplestone can count above four,' objected Joshua.

'Well, he never seems to know how many of us there are. He forgets whether there are four Smiths, or two Smiths, or three Smiths,' said James, 'because he asked me once, when we were out for a walk.'

'Anyway, Maria, I should go,' said Thomas, 'we'll keep him at bay for you, and as it's his last afternoon he won't have time to do much scolding.'

On Friday morning Maria kept up an endless 'shall I? shan't I?' debate with herself. But it was hopeless, she could not make up her mind. 'If I throw this rubber on to the floor,' she thought to herself, 'and it lands with the side up that has my initial written on it, I'll go, if not, not.'

'Maria is playing an elaborate game with herself,' said Mr Copplestone as she leant down from her chair to pick it up, 'with an indiarubber as a substitute for a ball. We will all pause and watch her, we may learn something.'

Flushed with embarrassment and stooping, Maria picked

up the rubber; her initials were on the top. Now she would have to go.

'Well, have you laid your plans, Maria?' Thomas asked, at the end of the morning's lessons. He was sitting on the edge of the table lazily watching James swing an ink pot round and round his head. Mr Copplestone had told them that if only they swung it round fast enough centrifugal force would keep the ink from falling out, and James wanted to see if it was true.

'I haven't laid any *plans*,' said Maria, with some alarm, 'I just thought I would go. I'm sure that ink on the wall must come from James, hadn't he better stop?'

'You must plan something, otherwise there'll be a fearful hue and cry here in the house and search parties sent out for you. If you didn't turn up for luncheon, for instance. I should think the best thing would be if you sloped off while we were having our walk, and then we could calm down the Streak by ourselves, and nobody need know.'

The gong boomed in the distance. James put down the inkpot. 'What the Streak said about liquid staying in if you swung it round isn't true – look at all that ink on the wall. I'll be the first person to be sitting down in the dining-room.' He rushed for the door. 'I promise I will, just you see.'

'Jas, you haven't washed your hands,' shouted Joshua after him.

'I wiped them on the tablecloth,' he called back, dashing across the landing and turning the corner to the last flight. 'Come on, you're supposed to be trying to race me. I can jump from the fourth step up now. Do you think when I'm a man I'll be able to jump from the top?' He landed on all fours at his father's feet, picked himself up, dodged round him, and the others could hear him slamming himself into his chair in the dining-room.

'James!' they all shouted. Jumping from the stairs was

strictly forbidden. Mrs Smith had once met somebody who had a niece who broke her nose doing this.

'Sorry, sorry, sorry!' he shouted back. 'I had to do it, I'd *sworn* I was going to be the first to sit, and if I'd broken my vow it would have been like breaking a promise. Wouldn't it, Papa? Papa, are women allowed in the Bodleian Library? because ...' But here Thomas tapped him severely on the shoulder. 'No liquorice for you,' he said.

'Women are allowed in Bodley,' said Professor Smith, 'much to the Librarian's disgust, he does everything he can to make things difficult for them. But because of what?'

'Oh, just because I wanted to know. Thos, you will give me the liquorice, won't you?'

'And where are we going to walk this afternoon?' asked Mr Copplestone afterwards, 'on this our last expedition together?'

Maria looked hopefully at Thomas. He played up. 'Can we go somewhere near a bookshop? There's some money I want to spend. I think Blackwell's would be best.'

'Is that Aunt Anna's half-crown you're going to spend?' demanded James. 'You've had it for years. I thought you were saving it for a real crisis. Don't let's go far, it's hot walking.'

'Half-crowns can be saved for too long,' said Mr Copplestone. ' "Lay not up for yourselves treasure upon the earth" etcetera, etcetera. We shall all spend Thomas's money for him.'

'All except you,' muttered Thomas to Maria. 'I hope you realize the sacrifice I am making for you.'

Maria ran back to the Lodgings to collect the piece of paper which, locked in her diary, contained the notes she had so far made on Stephen Fitzackerley. She rushed downstairs again with it folded tightly into the pocket of her dress, and then paused by the dining-room door. A smell of mutton and gravy from the Warden's luncheon still lingered in the air. She went in and made her way over to the engraving of Jerusalem House. She put her finger on the flight of steps that led down from the terrace. 'That's where the inscription is,' she said to herself, 'and nobody but Mr Copplestone and Thomas and I have seen it, and nobody knows about Stephen either – until I write about him.' At that moment there was a clatter of footseps outside. It was too late, she was trapped. In came Amy, with a trayful of glasses. 'Lawks, Miss Maria,' she said brightly. 'What do you come to be doing here? Are you hungry already? It's a long time to your tea, you know.'

Five minutes later the four children and Mr Copplestone were straggling slowly down Broad Street, trying to keep to the shadows. James was trotting beside Thomas and begging him to buy the liquorice boot-lace soon; Joshua was walking on ahead beside Mr Copplestone, feeling that he ought to try to be as nice as possible to him as it was his last day, and Maria was wandering behind them, by herself, looking at the Bodleian buildings at the bottom of the street, and wondering how easy it was going to be to make her escape. They reached the bookshop, and stood for a moment gazing in the window. Mr Copplestone took off his hat and fanned his face. 'Stifling heat,' he said. 'There will be a storm tonight, a very suitable end to my tutordom. And after all, didn't I prophesy a fortnight of fine weather? That fortnight is up today.'

Thomas jogged Maria's elbow. 'When are you going to go?'

'I'll go inside with you first,' she whispered back.

'Anything to gain time,' Thomas said scornfully, and he led the way in. The shop might have been specially designed to escape one's friends, with its dim lighting and many hidden corners. Mr Copplestone sniffed the air like a war-horse about to go into battle, and disappeared up a staircase, followed by James who was always eager to explore. 'Go on,' urged Thomas, giving her a push. And Maria walked out of the shop back into the oven-like heat of the street outside.

She ran over the gravel of the Bodleian quadrangle. There was no time to waste, because even if nobody came to look for her in the library, she must be back in the Lodgings in time for tea. She pushed shut the door, remembering that last time there had been a bull galloping about outside, and started to climb the staircase up to the library. When she rounded the first corner she caught sight of what seemed to be a very familiar back rounding the corner ahead. She stopped dead. 'Uncle Hadden,' she said to herself with horror. The footsteps of Uncle Hadden (if it was he) sounded now from the last flight of stairs. Well, I must make sure it is Uncle Hadden, thought Maria, and see where he goes to, so that I can avoid him. But when she reached the top of the stairs and, panting, pushed open the glass-topped door, he had disappeared. She tiptoed to the part of the library that Mr Evans had called Duke Humphrey. There was nobody to be seen except Mr Evans at his desk, writing furiously away as if the end of the world were at hand. So she went up to him scraping her feet noisily along the floor, and hoping that he would look up. He did not, so she coughed a little, and then said, 'Please, could I have the same book out as I had a few days ago?' Mr Evans started violently, and made a great ink blot over the spot where he had been writing. 'I haven't got to go and ask the Protobibliotecarius Bodleianus again, have I?' she added anxiously.

'No,' said Mr Evans grimly, 'I shouldn't do that. Your book may have been put aside among the reserved books, you had better look.'

'But I don't know where they are,' said Maria in great dismay. 'I don't know anything about anything here.' So Mr Evans, clutching his pen in his hand, and looking as though he were counting up the seconds that Maria was making him lose, came and found the book for her. Armed with it, she crept down the room, looking for a free desk and keeping a stealthy lookout for her uncle. But he was nowhere about. She settled down in one of the end recesses, and opened her book, and began to read the chapter she had begun earlier. There was a great deal to be read, for this Lord Fitzackerley seemed to have been the most famous and romantic figure of his family. He had not only gathered a circle of poets and writers round him at Jerusalem House, but had also written poems of his own, and composed songs. The book rambled on for page after page in its account of the people who had met at Jerusalem, and Maria felt obliged to read them carefully in case a reference to the children slipped in. Then the book moved on to the Civil War. Lord Fitzackerley had been a passionate supporter of the King against Parliament, and had fled to the Continent in 1652, to spend the rest of his life wandering round the courts of Europe, trying to beg help for the Stuarts. 'Oh, help,' muttered Maria as she took in the date. 'That throws everything out if none of the family were at the house in 1654, S. St G. F. couldn't have been Stephen Fitzackerley at all.' With sinking hope she plodded on, reading the letters that Lord Fitzackerley had written to his friends in England describing efforts to raise arms and men for the royal cause, letters to French and Dutch noblemen whom he thought might help. Then came her reward. The book finished with Sir Richard's wanderings, and turned to Jerusalem. 'During these years,' it said, 'the heir to the title had, it is to be presumed, remained alone at Jerusalem House with his tutor, who was also the domestic chaplain, and a handful of servants.' Then followed a letter from Lord Fitzackerley to the tutor asking about Stephen's well-being, for it seemed that the father, worried at the thought of the boy left alone in England, was also afraid that the tutor was too wrapped up in his own studies to pay much attention to the boy. An uncle was named, the Viscount Sissinghurst, the brother of Lord Fitzackerley's dead wife, who took an interest in the boy, and seemed to want to carry him away to his own house. But Stephen and his father were passionately determined that Jerusalem House should never be left without a Fitzackerley. Maria copied all this down as fast as she could. But then her pencil broke. With her hand aching from writing, she leant back in her chair and pushed the damp streaks of hair back from her forehead. There were pages more to get down, and she had no pencil and the crumpled piece of paper on which she had made her original notes would only take a few more sentences. She would never be able to come back again and finish off her work; the only thing to do was to go out now and buy some more writing materials.

It was as she came back into Duke Humphrey, rather blown from running so fast up the stairs, and still palpitating from the anxiety of wondering whether she was going to run into Mr Copplestone and the boys, that she saw the Warden. He was sitting with his head bowed over an enormous book, in the next recess to her, and in fact, if it had not been for the high bookcase, they would be sitting opposite each other. He did not lift his head as she slithered past and sat down in her own place. If she looked down under the table she could see his feet; it was a most uncomfortable situation. Supposing I kicked him by mistake and he came round to see who had done it? she thought, and immediately wound her feet round the chair legs to keep them out of danger. Then, with anxious pauses to listen to Uncle

Hadden's movements and to glance at his feet, she got to work again. She copied down various facts about the life of Lord Fitzackerley, for she hardly had enough facts about the boy alone to make a learned article. Indeed, after the letter to the tutor, the book had very little more to say about him. It turned to the uncle, Viscount Sissinghurst, and the rebellion he had tried to raise against Parliament. And then, at the very end of the chapter, after the death of Lord Fitzackerley in France was described (the unlucky man had died in exile, just before Charles II was restored to the throne), Stephen's name came up for the last time: 'Of the son, Stephen Fitzackerley, little more is known, except that he died before his father, in 1654, and the title then passed to a different branch of the family.' Nothing about how he died or where he was buried. Perhaps he had gone to France and died there, or perhaps he had been killed by Roundheads. But how was she going to find out more? There seemed to be no chance of taking the matter any further.

She sucked her pencil and stared out through the window into the tops of trees in a college garden below. She turned her head idly as she heard footsteps coming up the library, and with a jump of dismay saw the lean figure of the Librarian – the Protobibliotecarius himself – pass her and pause just beyond, where Uncle Hadden was sitting. He had not turned his head in her direction, but she could see his back now as they murmured together on the other side of the bookcase, and any moment now he might turn and recognize her and tell Uncle Hadden that she was there. She sat crunching her pencil between her teeth in alarm, looking wildly round her, and wondering how she could possibly escape. And then, out of the quiet and the peace of the library came a loud voice which drowned whatever the Librarian might be saying to the Warden. The situation was now even more horrifying than it had been a few seconds before, for the voice was the voice of Mr Copplestone. 'By thunder, it's Evans quartus, isn't it,' she could hear him saying. 'Warty quartus we used to call you twenty years ago.' Mr Copplestone's voice rose to a wail of reproach. 'My dear fellow, you *must* remember. Twenty years is a mere nothing, and I'm sure *I* have not changed. You certainly have not, you still have ink on your forehead, probably the same ink.' Mr Evans, however, did not seem to be behaving in the friendly way that Mr Copplestone had expected, and Mr Copplestone's voice became protesting. 'It's no good you saying you cannot help me. What is an official of the Bodleian for, may I ask, even such a one as old Warty quartus? What the Bodleian has done, my dear Warty, is to have kidnapped one of my pupils.' At this point, overcome with horror, and hardly knowing what she did, Maria plunged down on to her hands and knees under the table. Anything to avoid being discovered. The Librarian was striding off to rescue Mr Evans, and presumably everybody in the place was peering out from behind bookcases in the direction of Mr Copplestone. It was quite impossible to escape up that way. So Maria, not looking to right or to left, not thinking of anything except how urgent it was to get out of the library, went on crawling up the room under the tables and bookcases. She passed wastepaper baskets and feet, she had no idea whether anybody saw her – at least they didn't make a grab at her. Then when she came out from under the last table she got to her feet, and without looking at the angry group a few yards away – Mr Copplestone, Mr Evans, and the Librarian, all talking loudly at each other – she walked quickly past. Outside the swing door, stood Thomas, Joshua, and James, their faces pressed against the glass. 'I can't stop,' she said frantically as she pushed her way through the cluster. 'They're all after me.'

Mr Copplestone's voice became protesting

Thomas rose to the occasion. 'Go on, quickly then. Go back to our schoolroom. I'll tell the Streak that we've found you. Where is he?'

'You'll soon find him,' called Maria from the landing below. 'You can hear his voice all over the place.'

CHAPTER TWELVE

A Stolen Piece of Paper

Maria was sitting at the schoolroom table, pleating the tablecloth nervously between her fingers, when the others came in. Underneath her on the chair was the exercise book she had had to buy to take the rest of her notes. From time to time she tried to brush away the dusty marks she had made on her dress by crawling the length of the library.

'Ha!' said Mr Copplestone, breathing hard, and glaring at her fiercely. 'I shall never be able to enter Bodley again without various gentlemen throwing themselves into violent fits of rage. And you, madam, are responsible for this situation.'

'What about Maria?' asked James. 'Will she throw them into fits of rage?'

'Unfortunately,' said Mr Copplestone, 'among the wealth of angry words that have just been uttered, her name was never once mentioned. She was always referred to as "my pupil". It is a thoroughly unjust state of affairs.' He turned abruptly to Maria. 'I suppose it was this S. Fitzackerley that took you there? This S. Fitzackerley seems to be landing us in a great deal of trouble all round, to put it at its mildest.'

'Do you think you'll both have to go to prison?' James asked him eagerly.

'Maria will no doubt be sent to a reform school.'

Maria raised her head in great dismay. 'Uncle Hadden found out that I was there then?'

'Maria, you dunce,' muttered Thomas. 'He's not serious.'

'Serious?' said Mr Copplestone, overhearing part of what had been said. 'Of course it's serious. You disappear when you are in my charge. Two Smiths have no knowledge whatever of where you have gone, the third stubbornly refuses to tell me. We pace Broad Street distraught, by the mercy of heaven catch a sight of you, and then have to stalk you in a thoroughly undignified manner to the Bodleian where we turn the place upside down to find you –'

'It was lovely stalking you,' interrupted James. 'I wish we could do it every day.'

'And when we finally arrive in Duke Humphrey we are abused by every official in it, merely for inquiring after you. To think of that wretched little creature, Evans quartus, being in a position to lord it over me! The last time I saw him was when we were sailing his hat on the school pond.'

But the mention of his old school brought Mr Copplestone back to a good humour, and he spent what was left of the afternoon boasting about what he had done there, and also of what he had said to the Librarian to put him in his place. But when four o'clock struck and Maria began to gather her books, he said, 'One word of warning, madam, in case fate parts us for ever. Don't let zest for research, and for S. Fitzackerley, land you in any more criminal activity. It might be difficult to avoid the reform school without me to help you.' He peered out at the sky which was clouded over now with a grey haze. 'The thunderstorm is on its way, perhaps it will cool down tempers a little.'

As Maria sat that evening in her purple wallpapered room reading over the notes she had made, she thought wearily that there was no need for Mr Copplestone's warning; as far as she could see, there was no possibility of finding out anything more about Stephen Fitzackerley. Long before she could present her uncle with a history of his life, she would, as Mr Copplestone had warned her, be packed off to a reform school; it seemed easier to be good than to be clever – at least, when Mr Copplestone was out of the way. The Fitz-ackerleys had better be abandoned. She shut the exercise book and buried it deep in a drawer under her handkerchiefs and gloves.

The storm that Mr Copplestone had prophesied broke over Oxford that night, with colossal claps and cracks of thunder, and Maria lay with the bedclothes pulled over her head so that she would not see the lightning. She heard the clocks strike the quarters and the hours up to four o'clock, and then, when the thundering and crashing became more distant, she fell asleep. When she awoke it was raining steadily from a dull white sky; it seemed an entirely different world from yesterday. The rain fell almost continuously for five days, and the more it rained the further it seemed to take Maria from the extraordinary adventures and mishaps that had come their way while Mr Copplestone had been in charge. Mrs Clomper had never known such rain, she said, not in June, and she sat tight in her room, only emerging to scold Maria for spilling painting water over the table in her sitting-room or for jumping into the hall from the fifth stair up. The Warden was absorbed by examinations. Maria would see him setting off for the Examination Schools in white tie, cap and gown, and bringing other scholarly-looking men back with him at the end of the day. They splashed up Canterbury Lane together, their heads bent against the rain, and disappeared with him into the study for hours on end. Sometimes, to her embarrassment, they came out into the hall as she was passing, and then the Warden would say, 'My niece, Maria; Maria, these are Professors Blank and Blank.' She was always too nervous to catch their names. During this time she saw very little of her uncle and took her tea with Mrs Clomper. There did not seem to be much to talk about, though Mrs Clomper did sometimes speak of her sister-in-law who lived at Bicester and had a husband who grew giant vegetable marrows and runner beans as long as your arm.

Mr Ledgard returned to Oxford. He was standing in the schoolroom when Maria arrived for lessons on Monday, a small active man with a watchful eye. From the start he was able to quench James without bribes. James only tried 'But Mr Copplestone used not to . . .' once. Mr Ledgard just said, 'I am quite a different man from Mr Copplestone. I think it will save you a lot of trouble to remember this from the start.'

'It's hard work,' said Maria to Thomas after lunch on Tuesday, as they waited in the schoolroom before the afternoon walk. 'I feel out of breath, I've worked so hard. Does Mr Ledgard get angry if you don't know your lessons?'

'I've known him to,' said Thomas in a lofty way. 'But of course it's nothing to what will happen at Rugby.'

It was a dreary walk that day. None of them wanted to go out in the rain, and after they had tramped round North Oxford roads for half an hour, glumly following the black figure of Mr Ledgard, who was huddled under an enormous umbrella, they returned to the schoolroom and settled themselves round the table for the last lesson of the day.

Mr Ledgard had picked up the history book and was trying to find out just how far they progressed in it under Mr Copplestone. This was difficult because Mr Copplestone had never bothered much about history books, and they had jumped about the centuries, arguing about Bonnie Prince Charlie one day, and Guy Fawkes the next. Mr Ledgard looked up from the book with an impatient frown, to find that the children were not trying to remember whether they had covered the reign of Mary Tudor properly during the past weeks. They were sitting with strained expressions and half-guilty smiles, listening to sounds on the landing below. 'I'll go up myself, no trouble at all, no trouble at all,' said a voice cheerfully, and then came sounds of the stairs being taken two at a time, and somebody humming loudly. 'The Streak,' said James. Mr Ledgard opened his mouth to admonish them all, but there came a rap, and the familiar head of Mr Copplestone peered at them round the door.

'Well, *discipulae meae*, or should I say *discipulae Ledgardis*.' He bowed his head gracefully in Mr Ledgard's direction. 'How wags the world with you?'

There was silence in the schoolroom; the children looked at him uncertainly, and then at Mr Ledgard, who was frowning heavily. 'May I ask if you have a message for any of us? If not, I think we ought to proceed with our history lesson.'

'I have come up on a very frivolous pretext,' said Mr Copplestone, hanging his head and smiling at the door. 'It is merely to say good-bye to my former pupils, to whom I really became quite attached. I am off to Bolivia, you know, tomorrow morning,' he added as an afterthought.

Thomas rose to his feet, and the others followed suit, with a great clattering of chairs. 'Good-bye,' they all said. 'Thank you very much for taking us to Jerusalem House,' Joshua said politely. 'Why are you going to Bolivia?' demanded James.

'To study the customs of the inhabitants,' said Mr Copplestone. 'Shall I bring you back a llama apiece? Which reminds me, I had almost forgotten. I have brought something for Miss Maria. I think it ought to interest her more than anything else.' He came farther into the room, and delved in a pocket of his coat tails. 'Here you are,' he said, handing her a folded piece of paper, which seemed brown with age. 'I have an acquaintance by the name of Benson at Canterbury College, a sandy sort of man. I happened to find this lying on his desk when I called on him yesterday. I'm perfectly sure you have more right to it than he has.' Maria looked at the paper with a startled expression. 'Does he know you have given it to me?' she asked.

'Oh, no,' said Mr Copplestone airily, backing out of the room. 'He was unfortunately not there when I called. Good-bye, young Smiths, if you want to get in touch with me during the next three years you could always write care of the Post Office, La Paz. But I don't suppose any letters will reach me,' he added through the nearly closed door. And the children, still standing up, heard him running down-stairs.

'I don't know what that piece of paper may be,' said Mr Ledgard, 'but I think you had better put off reading it until this lesson is over. Now, will you turn to page 105 of your history books, and we will start at the reign of Edward VI.'

The folded paper lay in front of Maria for the next hour, and the four children furtively eyed it. But it was not actually opened until the Canterbury clock chimed the half hour for half past three, and Mr Ledgard had closed the history book. Then, as he shut the door of the schoolroom Maria seized it. The boys crowded round. She unfolded it nervously, for the paper seemed so brittle that she was afraid it would break at the folds. Inside there was writing in an ink that had faded to brown. But it was not difficult to read. At the top was written 'Paris, 24 april 1654'.

'It's two hundred and twenty years old,' said James with awe, jogging Maria's elbow violently in his excitement. 'It must be very valuable. What does it say? Maria, I can't see it if you hold it like that.'

'You'd better read it aloud,' said Thomas, 'Jas will tear it in pieces otherwise.'

' "My dear son," ' read Maria, ' "I am in haste, for one is waiting to carry this letter to England. I write to say that

I would have you portrayed by Mr Lely, that if aught befalls you in these sad times, there yet may hang in Jerusalem a picture of him who held the house against its enemies. I have sent word to Mr Lely to attend on you. Be sure that you have on you that gold chain that was your dead mother's. Let me hear of thy health which will ease the pain of this absence. Be thou still so religious that thy prayers may preserve from danger thy affectionate father, Fitzackerley."' Maria came to the end, and in a daze let the letter fall on the table. 'But this proves everything,' she said. 'That the drawing was by Lely, as the Streak said, that it is of Stephen Fitzackerley, that he wore a gold chain – everything.'

'Fancy the Streak finding a letter like that, which ought to be in a museum,' said Joshua.

'He didn't find it,' said Thomas, 'that's the point, he stole it. It's stolen property, and you'll have to give it back, Maria.'

'Stolen!' said the others, shocked.

'Of course it's stolen. Mr Copplestone took it from somebody's desk. You must take it back at once, Maria.'

'But where shall I take it to?' Maria asked miserably. 'It looks as though it's come from Jerusalem House. I can't take it there and give it to that dreadful Miss Hickmott.'

'You could post it,' suggested Joshua.

'Mr Copplestone didn't get it from Jerusalem. Weren't you listening. He said something about somebody called Benson of Canterbury.'

'He called him a sandy gentleman,' put in James. 'Does that mean he has sand all over him like sandpaper?'

'Oh, help,' said Maria, remembering, 'that's the man that pulled James out of the river and that knew my father. He said something about working on Fitzackerley family papers.'

'Then that makes it easier for you to give it back,' said Thomas. 'And James, don't try to be funny, it's just silly.'

'It makes it far more difficult. How can I say where I got it? Thos, won't you take it?' said Maria with beseeching eyes. 'Or couldn't I give it to somebody to deliver?'

'No, you can't. It was given to you and you must take it back. And today too, it's probably very valuable.'

'But what shall I say?'

'You'd better tell the truth. If Mr Copplestone is going to Bolivia tomorrow it won't matter to him.'

There was no help for it. Maria despairingly went to put on her coat. She came back to the schooolroom. 'Can I take a copy of it, then?'

Thomas hesitated. 'Oh, do let her, Thos,' said Joshua. 'Whatever does it matter?'

'It may matter a very great deal – copyright and so on. But still, I suppose she can if she tells this Mr Benson that she has.' She copied it down hastily on the back of her Greek exercise book. James leant over her shoulder. 'How funny only having a surname, do you suppose he wasn't christened, or something?'

'Oh, James, don't be a fool,' said Thomas. 'If you are a lord you only put your surname when you sign letters.'

James digested this. 'Then some day I'll probably be signing myself Smith.'

'I was waiting for you to say that,' said Thomas. 'Come on, Maria, hurry up.'

She looked up miserably. 'How do I find where Mr Benson lives?'

'Really, Maria,' he said impatiently, 'you're being a little weak in the head. Ask a porter, of course. Or do you want me to come with you?'

'Oh, Thos, please yes,' she begged. Thomas went to get his ulster.

The porter at the lodge directed them to the farther quadrangle. Maria dragged her feet over the wet paving stones and nervously fingered the paper in her coat pocket. 'Here we are,' said Thomas, peering at the number above a door that seemed to lead to a little turret. 'He's on the top floor of this staircase. Up you go, I'll wait in the doorway down here.'

Maria toiled up the spiral stone staircase, climbing round and round until she felt thoroughly giddy. At last she came to a door which had 'Mr Benson' painted on it. A low mutter was the only answer she got to her knock. After hesitating and wondering whether it meant 'come in' or 'go away', she pushed the door open and edged in, into darkness. There sat Mr Benson, in a circle of light thrown by the lamp on his desk. Heavy curtains were drawn across every window in the room. But more than the darkness Maria was amazed by the disorder of the room. Mr Benson's desk held dangerously high piles of books, which he would surely have to stand on a chair to reach. Round his chair were black tin boxes spilling out papers, so that he seemed to be held prisoner at his desk. But worse than any of this were the little heaps of papers that were clustered thickly all over the floor. They were weighted down by various things, a couple of shoes here and there, Roman-looking marble busts, a tea-cup, and three trays of half-eaten meals. Mr Benson did not raise his head. Maria advanced delicately between the objects on the carpet, and then came to a stop by a pile of papers that was kept down by a glass paperweight. Inside the weight was a picture of a kingfisher. She waited, but Mr Benson paid no attention whatsoever. So, feeling very bold, she bent down to examine the kingfisher. It was extraordinary how it ever got inside the glass, and she thought it would be interesting to break the weight and see what the picture was made from. But after she had seen as much as she wanted of the kingfisher she began to wonder what she ought to do next. The longer she stayed the more impossible it became to interrupt. Perhaps she could slip the paper on to the desk and creep out? She finally decided to do this, and tiptoed forward. But Mr Benson must have heard her rustling past the papers, because he said, without lifting his head, 'Gray, whatever you

He seemed to be held prisoner at his desk

do don't take those trays away. I know you're longing to, but don't. Utter chaos will follow. And Gray, bring me up a tray of supper tonight again. I shan't be dining in Hall.'

Maria was at a complete loss. 'I'm afraid . . .' she began. Mr Benson looked up abruptly. 'Well, save us! It's the Warden's niece, isn't it? How long have you been here?'

'Oh, not long,' said Maria hastily. 'I'm very sorry to interrupt you, but I thought I ought to give you back this.'

Perhaps, she thought, he would ask no questions, but just go on working. But this was too much to hope for. On seeing the paper Mr Benson gave a hoot of astonishment. 'And just how did you come by this?' he asked.

'It was given to me this afternoon, I don't know why, by Mr Copplestone. He said he had just called on you.'

'Oh, Copplestone,' said Mr Benson. 'There's no knowing what he'll do. We ought to form a league for the protection of the world against Copplestone. Well, I'm glad the paper reached your responsible hands.' There was a pause, and Maria turned to go. But Mr Benson proceeded. 'It's an odd thing that Copplestone should have given this paper to you of all people, because you were asking me about this very same Stephen Fitzackerley, weren't you? Now you're here you'd better see the other correspondence concerning him that I've come across since I have been going through the family papers.' He passed a weary hand over his forehead. 'The trouble is, heaven knows where they are now.'

'Shall I help you?' asked Maria, trying to conceal her excitement and impatience.

'No, no, by heaven no!' said Mr Benson, leaping up from his chair. 'Promise that on no account, whatever happens, will you touch any of these papers. They are exceedingly carefully arranged, and if they are disturbed in any way they will throw me into terrible confusion.'

'I promise I won't,' said Maria, backing towards the door in her alarm.

With his forehead furrowed in deep thought, Mr Benson crouched down on the floor, muttering to himself, and started rummaging under one of the trays. 'My scout will insist on trying to take these trays from me. He doesn't seem to realize that they are a vital part of my system. I remember the dates of the correspondence by what I have used to weight down the papers. Monday's tea-tray, for instance, covers the letters you want, I believe. Ah, here we are, there is not much, but you will see the reason why when you read them.' He handed Maria some papers. She looked at the top one. In faded brown ink she saw 'Jerusalem, 20 July 1654'. She recognized the date like a familiar friend; it was the date carved on the steps. Mr Benson tapped the paper. 'This letter and the one below it never reached their destination, the soldiers came too quickly.'

Maria read: 'My lord,' it began, 'my Lord Sissinghurst has sent word that soldiers are on their way to Jerusalem, and bids us fly now lest later we cannot. We leave in a few hours. Your lordship's humble servant, John Giles.' There was another letter underneath. 'It breaks my heart to leave Jerusalem to its enemies, but since you have commanded it, my dear father, and now my uncle Sissinghurst has sent urgent word that we leave without delay, we come. Adieu, my lord. Your loving son, Stephen Fitzackerley.'

Maria lifted her head. 'But I don't understand,' she said. 'What had happened?'

Mr Benson was carefully adjusting the various objects that weighted down the piles of papers on the floor. 'It's perfectly simple,' he said without turning round. 'Lord Fitzackerley seems to have been involved with his brother-in-law Sissinghurst in a plot against the Cromwell régime. He was probably supplying him with arms. He became afraid of the consequences for his son if the plot was discovered, and wrote to him to join him in France. (We know he was in France because there's a letter somewhere in one of these piles written from Paris about a portrait of the son which Lely was to do.) A few days after he had told his son to leave Jerusalem the plot was discovered, Sissinghurst realized that soldiers were on their way to Jerusalem, and sent an urgent message to the boy to leave at once with John Giles, who I suppose was the boy's tutor. But the letters never seem to have got sent. Perhaps the messenger who was to take them was killed, or perhaps they were forgotten in the flurry of the soldiers arriving.'

There was a moment's silence as Maria sorted this out, and fitted it to the facts she already knew. 'But what has happened to the father's letter telling Stephen to go, and why did you say that I would realize why there weren't any more letters?'

'Oh, didn't I give you that piece of paper?' Mr Benson fumbled again under Monday's tea-tray. 'Here you are.' It seemed to have been written in a great hurry. There were blots of ink on the paper, and the writing was crooked and smeared. 'I, Stephen Fitzackerley, on the day I leave this house, have destroyed all papers relating to my father, lest, innocent as they are, they should be used against him by his enemies. Jerusalem House, 20 July 1654.'

'Can I copy all these down?' asked Maria, 'and could I possibly borrow a pencil and some paper?'

'What was that you said?' Mr Benson who had by now reseated himself at his desk, wearily lifted his head. 'Copy them? By all means if you wish, I am not interested myself in the family at that date.'

'But what became of the boy?' Maria asked when she had copied down the three letters. 'The book said he died in 1654.' She was so excited by the new light that had just been thrown on the history of Stephen and his father that she forgot to care whether she was disturbing Mr Benson's concentration. There was no answer; Mr Benson was fathoms deep in thought. Maria went round the desk, and laying the papers beside him, repeated her question. He slowly raised his head and blinked at her. Maria suddenly remembered that you might do great injury to animals by disturbing their winter sleep of hibernation, and by waking up sleep-walkers, and wondered whether this applied to Mr

Benson. 'What became of the boy?' repeated Mr Benson slowly, coming back to the present with difficulty. 'I think you can take it that he went to France and died there soon afterwards.'

He tossed the papers into a black tin box on the floor, picked up his pen, and in a second again seemed completely unconscious of Maria's presence. She crept out of the room. At the bottom of the turret stairs Thomas was standing, the collar of his ulster turned up, morosely watching the rain beat up from the flagstones of the quadrangle. 'Maria!' he said angrily. 'You've kept me waiting here for exactly seventeen minutes. What on earth have you been up to?'

'Oh, Thos, I'm so sorry. But why did you go on waiting?'

'Of course I had to go on waiting. I said I would. I must say I was nearly coming up after you just now. I thought he must have thrown you out of the window or locked you up in a cupboard, or something. And then you just come coolly down and ask why I went on waiting. It's a bit too much, Maria.'

'You see, first he was working so hard that he wouldn't notice that I was in the room, and then he found me some terribly interesting letters which I had to copy – all about Stephen Fitzackerley. You know, Thos, it must have been Stephen who wrote "Begone, ye foul traitors". And now I know why, the soldiers were coming to the house and he couldn't do anything to them, except insult them like this. The dates fit and everything. He didn't want to leave the house but his father made him. It's so sad, don't you think. Oh, Thos, you're not listening.'

'Yes, I am listening. But I must say I don't care much about the Fitzackerley crew just now. I'm so hungry. Perhaps there'll be muffins for tea.'

CHAPTER THIRTEEN

The Warden Finds an Epitaph

THE trouble was that nobody seemed to care. It had always been Mr Copplestone who had taken the most active part in the research, and although so much of his help had been unwelcome, it had produced results. The Smiths were thoroughly bored with the whole affair by now, and tired of the name Fitzackerley. Maria longed to discuss it all with somebody, and hear other people's views on what had become of Stephen Fitzackerley, whether he had been killed by the Roundhead soldiers, or whether he had died in France. But it was impossible to confide anything to the Smiths these days; Thomas was very remote now that Rugby was nearly on him, and Joshua was thoroughly alarmed by the trouble the Fitzackerley affair had brought upon them all. James of course was hopeless. He was far too young, and anyway, he lived in a world of his own.

And so the article for which Maria had so painfully collected the facts never got written. The exercise book still lay buried under her handkerchiefs and gloves, together with the various notes she had taken from time to time, and every day the affair became more and more remote and the memory of that immensely hot fortnight with Mr Copplestone presiding over the schoolroom became a sort of dream. The Kips engraving of Jerusalem House was just a picture now, like the other pictures in the dining-room, and Maria could fix her eyes on it without any sort of memory of what had happened in the house or the garden. But sometimes, when she was least expecting it, when she was wandering in the college gardens, or walking round the Ashmolean Museum with Mrs Clomper, a smell of something old, scented, would come to her, a smell that vividly recalled Jerusalem House, and then she would feel sorry about that article that had never been written, and begin brooding again about what had become of Stephen Fitzackerley, who had died when he was so young, only three years older than herself, and one year older than Thomas. But there was not very much time for just thinking. Mr Ledgard worked them extremely hard, harder than Maria had ever been worked in her life before, and she was frightened of falling behind. She would spend the whole time between tea and supper struggling to bring sense into a Latin unseen, and drawing and re-drawing the diagram for a geometry problem in the hope that with a new diagram she could solve it; then she would fall wearily into bed.

And so the summer wore on. The university term was over long ago and the undergraduates gone; Oxford seemed very hushed and still. Their own holidays were starting on 27 July – 'The same day as Rugby,' said Thomas with satisfaction – and when Mr Ledgard returned in September it would be to teach only three of them, Thomas would have gone. Maria was not particularly looking forward to the holidays; Thomas and Joshua were going to be away, staying with cousins for the first half of August, and then the Smiths were all going down to Devonshire; and as the end of July came nearer she found herself dreading the next eight weeks. Whatever was she going to do with herself? Term finished, and she wandered round the Lodgings restless and miserable. Mrs Clomper said she was moping and her stomach must be out of order, and she dosed her with grey pills that Maria could not manage to swallow whole, and which tasted horrible when bitten. Even Uncle Hadden noticed after a few days. He put down *The Times* unexpectedly at breakfast one morning. 'Maria, my dear, he said, 'you seem unhappy. Is anything wrong?'

Maria hung her head. 'I'm very sorry,' she said humbly. 'There isn't anything wrong really.' But Uncle Hadden continued to look at her. 'Perhaps the Oxford air does not suit you. It certainly is rather trying in summer. How would it be if I were to send you away to the sea with Mrs Clomper for two or three weeks?'

To her horror Maria burst into tears. 'Oh, please, not. I like being in Oxford and being here. I'll get better, I promise.'

Uncle Hadden took off his spectacles and slowly began to rub them with an enormous red silk handkerchief. 'I think perhaps something should be done. You need a change of air, I fancy. But if you don't like the sea I shan't force it on you. My parents, I remember, thought that the sea air was essential to us children and were quite certain that we loved it. But how I hated it – a tearing east wind, and sand in my hair, and being obliged to bathe.'

But the threat that she might be sent away with Mrs Clomper hung over Maria and made her more miserable. She sat up in the pear tree and listened to the busy sounds of people running round the Smiths' house packing and preparing for the annual departure of the household to Devonshire for four weeks. She heard the agitated voice of Mrs Smith counting trunks and asking if this or that vital object had been packed, and if so, where. Then the faint sounds of voices from the street as the professor and Mrs Smith and James and the maids and the baggage (Thomas and Joshua were to join them in Devonshire) packed themselves into two cabs and departed for the station. After the cabs had rattled away over the cobbles the windows were bolted and the doors barred and curtains drawn by the woman who was going to feed the chickens and the pet rabbit while the Smiths were away, and then there was silence. Maria felt she had sunk to the last depths of depression, and wandered in to lunch wondering whether anybody had ever felt so miserable.

Not a word was said over luncheon until they had finished their soup. Then, as they sat waiting for Amy to bring in the meat, the Warden spoke. 'Maria,' he said, 'I have a suggestion to make. Mrs Clomper wishes to go on a long visit to her sister-in-law, and I am going to stay with a very old friend of mine, a widowed lady, at her country house in Kent. It occurs to me that you might care to come with me. I think you might quite enjoy yourself. The house has a river running through the grounds, and there is a farm, and an old pony to drive. I dare say Mrs Lacey will be able to produce some other children for you to play with too, if that is what you want. Would you care to come?'

'I think it would be lovely!' said Maria.

And so the Lodgings too were closed, and Uncle Hadden and Maria left Oxford on a hot August day, and after crossing London, jolted down through Kent in a pleasantly slow train, past hopfields and orchards and oasthouses. Mrs Lacey's house seemed, to someone who was used to the Canterbury Lodgings and their dark panelling and small windows, full of light. The windows reached almost to the ground, so that you could step out into the garden from any downstairs room, and the garden itself was mostly grass and trees, and sloped down to a river. Here Maria spent a lot of time, lying in the old punt that was moored under some trees. She read – there were books in every room of the house – or she just lay dabbling her feet in the water, gazing at the dazzle of leaves overhead. Or she watched them milk at the farm, or rode round the fields on the reaper.

Uncle Hadden took long walks by himself, and was often away for the whole day, but Mrs Lacey was very interesting company. For one thing, she was an amateur historian, with a great passion for the history of Kent, and particularly of that district where she lived, so that she could explain how the local inns got their names, what the village had looked like four hundred years ago, and tell the highly colourful histories of the local families. In the evenings Maria pored over the books that were too heavy to take in the garden to read during the day, tall volumes of engravings of buildings and towns in Kent, and lavishly illustrated travel books. They often played snap, or a racing game called Minarou, on which the Warden would make enormous bets with haricot beans, usually having to borrow from Maria to pay his way. If she had been a boy, he said, he would have considered it a most unsuitable game, likely to make for bad habits at the university, but he did not think that young women were ever tempted into gambling and horse racing.

And Maria began to remember the Fitzackerleys with interest. She had at the last minute thrown the exercise book and the documents into the trunk that Amy was packing for her. She thought about them as she lay in the punt with the sun falling on her in dapples through the leaves of the willow tree overhead, and then one day she brought down the material and started to re-read it. She no longer thought of presenting it to her uncle as a proof that she was not a hopeless failure, but she did feel that it was a pity, after so much trial and tribulation, to leave it there under her handkerchiefs and gloves. She thought she had collected enough facts to write quite an interesting account of Stephen Fitzackerley, and she could make it longer by adding some bits about the life of his father which she had found in the family history. She knew that Stephen St

George Fitzackerley had been born in 1640 and had been brought up at Jerusalem House, surrounded by poets and learned men, so that he was probably a very clever child. His mother had probably died when he was still a baby, for in the picture that was painted of him and his sister, he wore a gold chain that was later described as belonging to his dead mother. His sister Deborah died in 1652, when she was ten. (She could put in a description here of the picture which showed her holding a cockatoo.) After the outbreak of the Civil War the children's father, passionately Royalist, had fled to the Continent, leaving the boy Stephen alone at Jerusalem with his tutor, John Giles. (How terribly lonely it must have seemed then, Maria thought, remembering the vastness of the house and the gardens. And how unhappy the boy must have felt, wandering round the silent emptiness of the rooms which he had known when they were filled with guests and conversation and laughter. And he would always be thinking of his father, and whether he would ever again see him, and of how little he could do to save the house if the Roundheads decided to come down upon it.) In April 1654, Lord Fitzackerley, realizing that there was no picture of his son since he had been painted with his sister at the age of about six, had written that he wished him to be portrayed by Lely. A drawing had been made, and this now hung in Lady Margaret's Gallery at the house. A couple of months later, Lord Fitzackerley, who was engaged in a plot against the government with his brother-in-law, Lord Sissinghurst, thought that the situation was becoming too dangerous for Stephen to stay at Jerusalem, and seemed to have written to him telling him that he must join him in France. This letter had now been destroyed. But the plot was discovered, Lord Sissinghurst had word of the discovery, and sent a message to Stephen that he must not delay his departure but leave at once for the Continent. This message could only have come a day or so after the letter from Lord Fitzackerley, for Stephen had written to his father, that he must come at once, for his uncle had warned him that soldiers were advancing against the house. He and the tutor had left the house in great haste, but before he set off, he had had time to destroy all the letters from his father that he thought might be dangerous, and to carve a message to the soldiers defiantly in the stone. Only perhaps his courage had failed him, for the inscription on the garden steps might easily not have been seen by the soldiers. I expect what it was, thought Maria, was that he wanted to do something to show he had defied the soldiers, but he was afraid that if they were made angry they would wreck the house, and he did so love it. And so on 20 July 1654, he had ridden away from Jerusalem, and what had become of him nobody seemed to know. 'If only I could find out,' said Maria to herself. 'It's so sad not knowing when you're fond of a person.'

Her mind was on Stephen Fitzackerley that night, and she did not talk very much at dinner or over the game of Minarou. Uncle Hadden and Mrs Lacey were speaking of some lecture that she wanted him to give to the Kentish Historical Association.

'I know it's tricky,' Mrs Lacey was saying. 'On the one hand you have some very distinguished and learned historians in the audience, and on the other, mere dabblers like myself. And of course, they do like to hear about local history – they're very loyal to Kent, I think they even wish they could have a Kent National Anthem to start the proceedings. Well, you may get an idea for a talk on your drive tomorrow.' Mrs Lacey turned to Maria. 'I am sending you out with your uncle on a trip of exploration in the pony trap tomorrow. It's time you saw something of Kent, and I have a sewing meeting at the Rectory that will take up all the afternoon. I'll think of you inspecting graveyards while I'm stitching away at shirts for little black boys.'

So the next day, with their tea packed up beside them, they set off in the old pony trap with Rufus, the fat chestnut pony, who was also used, wearing special leather shoes, to pull the mowing machine. The Warden drove, which meant that he let the reins lie slack on Rufus's back while he read a book on his knee. He said that he had always got into trouble with his father's groom for doing this when he was a boy, and so the pleasure of it had never died, even after he had grown up. But then he became so absorbed in his book that he did not notice that Rufus had stopped dead and was devouring cow parsley from the side of the lane. So Maria asked if it would not be better if she took over and then he could read more peacefully. After that they drove fairly briskly through the sunny afternoon, and Rufus clip-clopped smartly along the roads that wound over the hills overlooking the great stretch of the Weald. And then they drove down into the Weald itself, rich with orchards and black and white cottages. They got out of the trap several times to inspect churches and wander through the long grass of the graveyards. Imitating Thomas, Maria had brought a note-book to copy down epitaphs. The one that pleased her most was one discovered by her uncle:

In seven years time there comes a change
Observe and here you'll see
On that same day come seven years
My husband's laid by me.

'Oh, but the poor thing,' said Maria. 'He had to wait seven years by himself.'

'Perhaps he had daughters,' said the Warden. 'Shall we have our tea under the lime trees?'

Mrs Lacey's cook had packed cucumber sandwiches, and walnut bread, and coffee cake, and, in a cabbage leaf, some of the yellow raspberries for which the kitchen garden was famous. When they had finished they decided to go home by a roundabout route. Their way lay through a different type of country, wooded and gently sloping, with great tree-shadowed meadows on either side of the road. 'Oh, look!' said Maria, letting the reins drop on Rufus's neck, and staring over the road. There, a few hundred yards away, with the setting sun bright on it, was a wonderful building, half house, half castle, piled on top of a grassy hill. 'Do you think we could go closer to have a look?'

The Warden saw no reason why not, and so she turned Rufus and the pony trap up the lane that led off the road up to the house. On one side was a field with the shadows lying long over it, on the other a high stone wall.

'There's a little church at the top of this lane, I see,' said the Warden. 'Shall we go up and see it? I'm afraid the best view of the house was from the road where we were, this wall prevents you from seeing much of it from the lane.'

They left the trap and walked up the lane. Rooks swept over their heads and cawed and fluttered among the tops of the elm trees in the field. They had hardly gone a few paces when Maria saw an iron gate in the wall. She ran over and peered through its rusty scroll work. From behind came a waft of heavy perfume; pinks perhaps. Hardly knowing what she did, she pushed open the gate. She wandered up a broad grassy strip between two flower beds. The smell of the flowers seemed to recall something to her; she frowned as she tried to remember. Then she lifted her head and said aloud, 'Stephen.' As she said it she looked expectantly round, as though he might appear. But that was only for an instant, for then the sound of her own voice in the hot empty garden startled her, and she took fright and ran back to the gate.

She caught her uncle just outside the little church. 'Did you manage to catch a glimpse of the house?' he asked. 'Come and look at the church; I have found an inscription which might interest you. It's to a boy who died young.'

'It's to Stephen Fitzackerley,' said Maria instantly.

Only once before could she remember ever seeing her

She wandered up a broad grassy strip

uncle surprised, and that was when she had told him she wanted to learn Greek and Latin. 'You have seen the inscription already then?'

'No,' said Maria in an embarrassed way. 'But I just thought he would be buried here.'

'Now that is very remarkable,' said the Warden, leading the way into the church, 'because I was wondering why he should be buried here. The Fitzackerley seat is Jerusalem House. This house must be the seat of the Viscounts Sissinghurst, the church is full of their tombs. This boy of yours is buried among them.'

The tablet to the memory of Stephen Fitzackerley was high on the wall of the chapel where the viscounts and their families were buried. The Warden pointed up to it. 'Here is the inscription,' he said, 'part of it is in Latin, see if you can read it.'

'"Stephen Fitzackerley,"' read Maria, '"of Jerusalem House in the county of Oxford. Born 25 March 1640. Died 22 July 1654, of a fall from his horse."' So he had died there, near his uncle's house, two days after he had left Jerusalem, when he was still only fourteen.

The Warden read aloud the inscription that followed. How rich and how sad the Latin words sounded, Maria thought, addressed to somebody so young. '"*Eruditione varia et praecoci virtutibus multis et mirandis ornatus; spem amantis patris vanam mors effecit improba et improvisa, cui manet desiderium non in hoc saeculo satiabile.*" He seems to have been a most remarkable boy. Can you understand what it says?'

'Great learning and many virtues,' stumbled Maria; but she had to give it up and the Warden translated for her: 'Precociously gifted with wide-ranging learning, and possessed of extraordinary virtues, death unforeseen and untimely disappointed the hopes of his loving father, whose grief cannot be assuaged.' He paused. 'I wonder what the history of that boy was, and how he comes to be buried among strangers.'

'But they weren't strangers; Lord Sissinghurst was his uncle. I'm glad he didn't go to France,' said Maria, almost forgetting that her uncle was standing beside her, as she tried to piece together in her mind the last two days of Stephen's life. He left Jerusalem House on 20 July, he must have been riding towards the coast to embark for France when he had been killed. 'Would there be time for me to copy it down?' she asked. 'I've got my epitaph book in the trap.'

The Warden watched her writing down the English and then the Latin. He was silent until she had finished. 'So you know the history of this boy, Maria. Did you discover it on one of your expeditions to Jerusalem?'

This was not how Maria had ever thought the story would be told. In her first enthusiasm she had pictured herself laying a printed article on the Warden's desk, and triumphantly proving to him that bad at maths as she might be, and disliked by Mrs Clomper, she still was worth educating. But she had given up all thought of that when she found it led to house-breaking, playing truant, gatecrashing into the Bodleian, and being a receiver of stolen property. Nevertheless, she told her uncle the whole story as they jogged home together in the pony trap. He listened without interrupting. 'This is most interesting, Maria,' he said at the end, 'and most creditable. I should think few scholars have so many obstacles thrown in the way of their research. And it makes an exceedingly interesting history.' He paused, with his head sunk down on his chest and his lips pursed. Then he went on. 'It seems just the sort of paper to deliver to the Kentish Historical Association – Mrs Lacey was talking about it last night, if you remember. It's certainly far more interesting than anything I could tell them, and the fact that this boy died among them, so to speak, gives it the right local colour.'

Maria was astounded. 'But they wouldn't want to hear me,' she said.

'They would rather hear a child-prodigy than an elderly man.' The Warden smiled. 'And if you feel the paper is rather short, you can tell your audience what it feels like to crawl out of the Bodleian Library, past the Librarian, on your hands and knees.'

'However much I wanted to know something,' said Maria with great emphasis, 'I could never go through that again. And I'd rather know nothing at all than have Mr Copplestone finding out things for me.'

When Marnie Was There

JOAN G. ROBINSON

Brooding, lonely Anna, a foster-child, goes to stay with a kind Norfolk couple. There, like something in her memory, she finds the old house backing on to the creek. But it is the girl at the window who haunts her . . . Marnie, headstrong, often infuriating and somehow just as elusive when the two meet as she had been at the window. Marnie becomes Anna's perfect friend, and though she finally vanishes for good, she has helped Anna to make real friends.

This is a thrilling, intense story, part mystery, part adventure, part fantasy, and will appeal particularly to girls of eleven and upward.

Thursday's Child

Noel Streatfeild

'Noel Streatfeild's position in the children's book world is unique. She has had all the accolades: a Carnegie Medal, a Bodley Head Monograph—and both critical and popular esteem . . . She is endlessly inventive, full of verve and real understanding of the surfaces of childhood.'

Times Literary Supplement

'The past comes to life with humour and grace in *Thursday's Child*', a period piece set at the turn of the century. Margaret Thursday makes a splendid heroine . . . A whole way of life springs brilliantly to life.' *Growing Point*

'Authenticity blends beautifully with romance . . . Children will love it.' *Daily Telegraph*

Thursday's Child 'promises to be a minor classic and it is enchantingly and appropriately illustrated by Peggy Fortnum.'

Birmingham Post